REA

®
teach
yourself

excel 2007

excel 2007

moira stephen

for over 60 years, more than
50 million people have learnt over
750 subjects the **teach yourself**
way, with impressive results.

be where you want to be
with **teach yourself**

For UK order enquiries: please contact Bookpoint Ltd, 130 Milton Park, Abingdon, Oxon OX14 4SB. Telephone: +44 (0)1235 827720. Fax: +44 (0)1235 400454. Lines are open 09.00–17.00, Monday to Saturday, with a 24-hour message answering service. Details about our titles and how to order are available at www.teachyourself.co.uk.

For USA order enquiries: please contact McGraw-Hill Customer Services, PO Box 545, Blacklick, OH 43004-0545, USA. Telephone: 1-800-722-4726. Fax: 1-614-755-5645.

For Canada order enquiries: please contact McGraw-Hill Ryerson Ltd, 300 Water St, Whitby, Ontario L1N 9B6, Canada. Telephone: 905 430 5000. Fax: 905 430 5020.

Long renowned as the authoritative source for self-guided learning – with more than 50 million copies sold worldwide – the **teach yourself** series includes over 500 titles in the fields of languages, crafts, hobbies, business, computing and education.

British Library Cataloguing in Publication Data: a catalogue record for this title is available from The British Library.

Library of Congress Catalog Card Number: on file.

First published in UK 2007 by Hodder Education, 338 Euston Road, London NW1 3BH.

First published in USA 2007 by The McGraw-Hill Companies Inc.

The **teach yourself** name is a registered trademark of Hodder Headline.

Computer hardware and software brand names mentioned in this book are protected by their respective trademarks and are acknowledged.

The publisher has used its best endeavours to ensure that the URLs for external websites referred to in this book are correct and active at the time of going to press. However, the publisher has no responsibility for the websites and can give no guarantee that a site will remain live or that the content is or will remain appropriate.

Typeset by MacDesign, Southampton

Printed in Great Britain for Hodder Education, a division of Hodder Headline, 338 Euston Road, London NW1 3BH, by Cox & Wyman Ltd, Reading, Berkshire.

Hodder Headline's policy is to use papers that are natural, renewable and recyclable products and made from wood grown in sustainable forests. The logging and manufacturing processes are expected to conform to the environmental regulations of the country of origin.

Impression number   10 9 8 7 6 5 4 3 2 1

Year   2011 2010 2009 2008 2007

contents

preface

Welcome to *Teach Yourself Excel*.

If you need to produce budgets, forecasts, summary data, statistics, financial information, charts or lists of data you'll find all the features you require in Excel.

This book will help you to unleash the power of Excel, quickly and painlessly. We start by introducing the basic skills that are needed to create and format a workbook attractively. Simple formulas and sophisticated formatting options will help to ensure that your worksheets are not only accurate, but look good too!

We then move on to introduce the many different and powerful functions that are available in Excel. Logical, statistical, math, text, date, financial and lookup functions are discussed.

Other features covered include charting and drawing, styles and templates, list management, macros, integration of Excel with other applications, sending worksheets by e-mail and preparing web pages in Excel.

Excel is a very powerful spreadsheet package – but don't let that put you off. You'll be amazed at what can be achieved easily!

I hope that you enjoy using this book and that it helps you to learn to use Excel.

Moira Stephen

2007

01

getting started

In this chapter you will learn:

- what you need to run Excel 2007
- how to install the software
- how to start Excel
- about the Excel screen and its tools
- how to use the Help system

1.1 Introducing Excel

Excel is a very powerful spreadsheet package – but don't let that put you off! You can use Excel to produce simple spreadsheets to help you prepare your invoices, budgets and summary statements. You can also use Excel to chart your data, manipulate it using database-type features and publish your worksheet to the Web. Excel integrates well with the other packages in Microsoft Office and you'll find out how you can use this to your advantage. Finally, Excel is very web-orientated – you'll soon be able to hyperlink to other files and Internet addresses, send e-mails and publish your worksheets and charts on the Web!

It is assumed that you have a working knowledge of Windows.

1.2 System requirements

These hardware and software specifications are for Office 2007. The recommended configuration is a PC with a minimum of a 500 MHz processor, 256 MB of RAM and 1.5 GB disk space. The minimum specification is given in the table below.

Processor	500 MHz or higher
Memory	256 MB RAM or higher
Hard disk	1.5 GB. A portion of this will be freed after installation if the installation files are removed from the hard drive.
Drive	CD-ROM or DVD drive
Display	1024 × 768 or higher resolution monitor
Operating system	Windows XP with Service Pack 2, Windows Server with Service Pack 1, or later system
Other	Certain features, e.g. inking, speech recognition, Information Rights Management have specific requirements – check out the Microsoft website.
Browser	Internet Explorer 6.0 or later, 32 bit browser only.

1.3 Installing Excel

To install Microsoft Office, follow the on-screen instructions.

1 Insert the CD into the CD drive.

♦ The CD will launch automatically, and the setup begin.

2 At the **Setup** dialog box, enter the 25-character product key.

3 For the user information, enter your name, initials (optional) and organization (optional).

♦ Your name will be used in the Author box in the Properties dialog box in the Office programs.

4 Read the End-User License Agreement and select *I accept the terms …* (if you don't agree, you can't continue!).

5 Select the type of installation.

6 At the final Setup stage, select the options and you're done!

1.4 Starting Excel

1 Click the **Start** button on the Taskbar.

2 Point to **All Programs.**

3   Select **Microsoft Office**.

4   Click **Microsoft Office Excel 2007**.

Which Office suite?

Excel is present in all eight editions of the Office 2007 suite. If you want to know what products are present in the different editions, visit http://www.microsoft.com.

1.5 The Excel screen

When Excel starts, you are presented with a new workbook displaying a blank worksheet. We'll take a tour of the Excel screen, so that you know what the various areas are called. You'll find the different screen areas referred to by the names given below in the on-line Help and throughout this book.

Application Minimize, Maximize and Close buttons

Application title bar

Workbook control buttons

Ribbon showing Home tab

Help

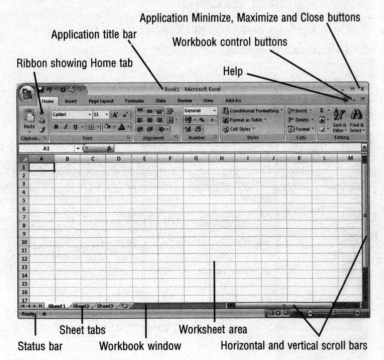

Sheet tabs

Worksheet area

Status bar

Workbook window

Horizontal and vertical scroll bars

If the workbook window is maximized, the workbook and the application windows share one title bar containing the application and workbook names.

1.6 Workbooks and worksheets

When working in Excel, the files that you create and work with are called *workbooks*. Each workbook consists of a number of *worksheets* – the default number is three. A worksheet is the primary document, and consists of cells organized into rows and columns. You can add, delete, move, copy and rename the worksheets, depending on your work requirements.

Related data is usually best kept on separate worksheets within the same workbook – this makes it easier to find and manage your data. For example, if you were collating regional sales figures, you could record the figures for each region on a separate sheet in the same workbook. Alternatively, you could have a workbook for each region and record the monthly or quarterly sales figures on separate sheets in each region's workbook.

Worksheets will be discussed more fully in Chapter 4.

1.7 Ribbon and tabs

The Excel features and commands are displayed on the Ribbon along the top of the worksheet area. The Ribbon is divided into task-orientated tabs, where the commands and features required to perform different tasks are grouped together e.g. the **Insert** tab has all the objects you might want to insert.

+ You can hide or restore the Ribbon by pressing [Ctrl]-[F1].
+ Click any tab to display it temporarily when the Ribbon is hidden.

Program tabs replace the standard tabs when you perform certain tasks, e.g. Print Preview.

Groups and command buttons

The command buttons on each tab are arranged in groups, e.g. the **Insert** tab has all the command buttons grouped together into areas – shapes, tables, illustrations, charts, links and text.

Microsoft Office button

The Microsoft Office button is located at the top left of the Excel screen. When clicked it displays a menu that gives you access to all the things that you can do with your file e.g. print, save, open, send.

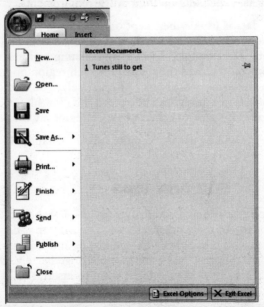

1.8 Quick Access toolbar

The Quick Access toolbar contains commands that are regularly used, and are independent of the tab being displayed. The toolbar can be displayed in one of two positions:

*   Above the Ribbon, beside the Microsoft Office button (the default position).

*   Below the Ribbon.

To move the Quick Access toolbar from one position to the other, click the arrow at its right and select **Place Quick Access Toolbar below the Ribbon** or **Place Quick Access Toolbar above the Ribbon** as required.

You can customize the Quick Access toolbar in the **Excel Options** dialog box.

1 Click the arrow at the end of the toolbar and select **Customize Quick Access Toolbar...**

Or

2 Click the Microsoft Office button then the **Excel Options** button.

3 At the **Excel Options** dialog box, in the **Customize** options, add or remove tools as required.

4 Click **OK**.

You can also add a command to the Quick Access toolbar directly from the Ribbon.

1 Right-click on the command you wish to move.

2 Click on **Add to Quick Access Toolbar**.

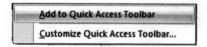

1.9 Dialog box launchers

Dialog box launchers are small buttons that appear at the bottom right of some groups.

Clicking a launcher opens a dialog box that displays more options related to the group.

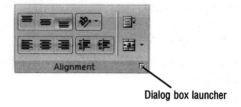

Dialog box launcher

1.10 Ribbon keyboard shortcuts

If you prefer to issue commands using the keyboard, Excel will automatically prompt you as you work.

1 Hold down the [Alt] key – and keep it down throughout the procedure.

* A 'ghost' letter appears next to each tab on the Ribbon.

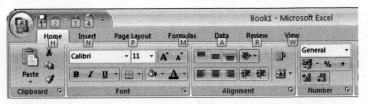

2 Press the letter key to activate the tab you want to use.

* Ghost letters/numbers will appear next to each command.

3 Press the letter/number to select the command button.

4 Release [Alt].

1.11 Help

As you work with Excel you will probably find that you need Help from time to time. To access the Help system:

* Click the **Help** button to the right of the ribbon tabs.

Or

* Press [F1].

To browse through the Help pages, click on any feature in the Help window.

Use the Help toolbar as you work in the Help pages.

From left to right the tools are:

* Back
* Forward
* Stop

- ◆ Refresh
- ◆ Home
- ◆ Print
- ◆ Change Font Size
- ◆ Show/hide Table of Contents
- ◆ Keep on top/Not on top.

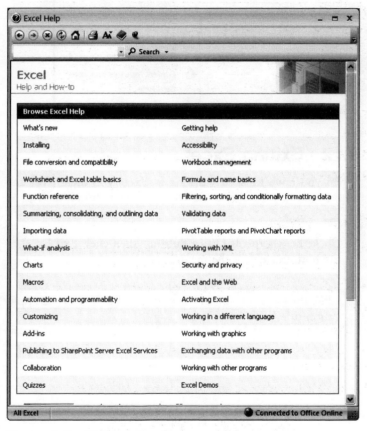

To search for Help on a topic:

1 Enter details of what you are looking for in the **Search** field.

2 Click **Search**.

Or

- Click the search drop-down arrow and select a search area.

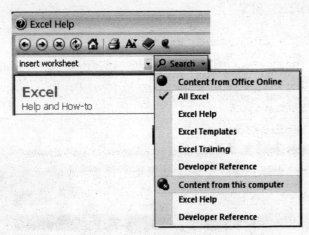

1.12 Exiting Excel

When you have finished working in Excel you must close the application down – don't just switch off your computer.

To exit Excel:

1 Click the Microsoft Office Button then click **Exit Excel** at the bottom right of the menu.

Or

2 Click the **Close** button in the right-hand corner of the application title bar.

Summary

In this chapter we have discussed:

+ The minimum software and hardware requirements

+ The installation procedure

+ Starting Excel

+ The Excel screen

+ The difference between workbooks and worksheets

+ The Ribbon and its tabs

+ The Quick Access toolbar

+ Dialog box launchers

+ Choosing commands using the keyboard

+ The Help system

+ Exiting Excel.

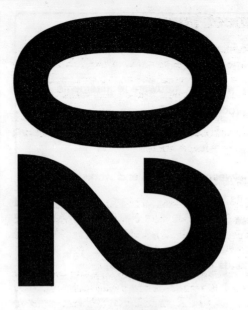

02

basic excel skills

In this chapter you will learn:

- some spreadsheet jargon!
- about workbooks
- about entering and editing text, data and formulas
- about formatting cells
- how to move and copy data and formulas

2.1 Spreadsheet jargon

This chapter will introduce you to the basic skills you will need to work in Excel. By the time you have completed this chapter you will have created a simple worksheet and you will know how to create, edit, save, print, open and close a workbook.

Before going any further, spend a little time getting familiar with some of the jargon you will encounter. There's nothing difficult about it – once you know what it means!

Rows, columns and cells

The worksheet area consists of rows, columns and cells. Rows are identified by the numbers down the left side of the worksheet area. Row 7 is highlighted in the illustration below. There are *lots* of rows on a worksheet – 1,048,576 in fact!

Columns are identified by letters displayed along the top of the worksheet area. Column E is highlighted in the illustration. After Z, columns are labelled AA to AZ, then BA to BZ, and so on to XFD, giving 16,384 columns in all.

Where a row and column intersect you have a cell. Each of the rectangular areas on your worksheet is a cell. Cells are identified using a cell *name* or *address*. A cell address consists of the column letter followed by the row number of the column and row that intersect to create the cell.

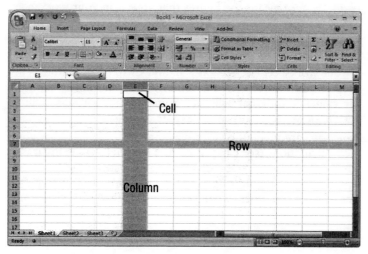

Cell A1, B9, C3, D6 and F3 have been highlighted in the screenshot below.

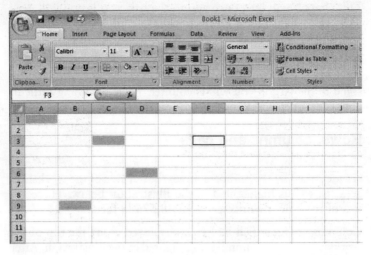

Text, data, formulas and functions

The cells in your worksheet will eventually contain text, numeric data, formulas or functions.

Text is used for titles or narrative to describe the figures that you are presenting. Worksheet headings, column headings and row labels will usually be text entries.

Numeric data means the figures that appear in your worksheet. The data may be entered through the keyboard, or it may be generated as the result of a calculation.

Formulas are used to perform calculations on the numeric data in your worksheet (see section 2.10 and Chapter 5). Formulas are used to add the value in one cell to that in another or multiply the values in different cells, etc. Some of your formulas will be very basic while others may be quite complex.

Functions are predefined formulas that perform simple or complex calculations (see Chapters 5 and 6). There are many different kinds of functions set up in Excel – statistical, logical, financial, database, engineering – and many more. You're bound to find some useful ones, whatever type of data you work with.

2.2 File handling

In Excel, a file is called a workbook. Each new workbook you create is automatically given a temporary filename – *Book1*, *Book2*, etc. The name appears on the workbook title bar.

When you open Excel a new workbook is created automatically. There are several ways in which you can create new workbooks and open existing ones in Excel.

New workbook

To create a new blank workbook:
1 Click the Microsoft Office button, then click **New...**
2 At the **New Workbook** dialog box, in the Templates categories, select **Blank and Recent** then **Blank Workbook** from the options.
3 Click **Create**.

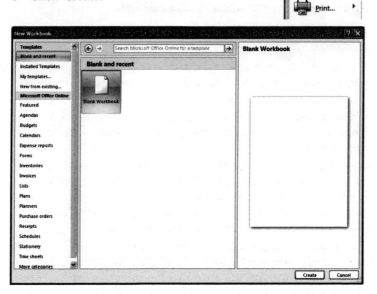

Or

• Press **[Ctrl]-[N]** to create a new blank workbook without opening the dialog box.

To create a workbook based on a workbook or template:

1 Click the Microsoft Office button, then click **New...**

2 At the **New Workbook** dialog box, select the **Template** category required.

3 Locate the workbook or template.

4 Click **Create**.

Open a workbook

To open an existing workbook:

1 Click the Microsoft Office button, then click **Open...**

♦ Or press [Ctrl]-[O] to display the **Open** dialog box.

2 Locate and select the workbook required.

3 Click **Open**.

Recently used files are listed to the right of the Microsoft Office button menu – to open one simply click on it.

Open

Look in: [Excel 2007 ▾] ⊙ · ▣ | ✕ ▣ ▦ ·

My Recent Documents
Desktop
My Documents
My Computer
My Network Places

📁 Chapter1
📁 Chapter2
📁 Teach Yourself Examples

File name: [▾]
Files of type: [All Microsoft Office Excel Files ▾]

Tools ▾   Open ▾   Cancel

Save a workbook

At some stage you must save your workbook to disk (if you don't you will lose it when you switch off your computer). When you save your workbook, you should give it a file name that reflects its contents rather than use the *Bookx* temporary name.

To save your workbook:

1 Click the Microsoft Office button, then click **Save As...**

2 At the **Save As** dialog box, locate the folder into which you wish to save your workbook (usually *My Documents* or a sub-folder).

3 Enter the name in the **File name:** field.

4 Leave the **Save as type:** at *Excel Workbook*.

5 Click **Save**.

You are returned to your workbook. Its name appears on the workbook title bar.

♦ The keyboard shortcut for **Save As...** is **[F12]**.

You can save your workbook at any time – you don't need to wait until you've entered all your data. I suggest you save your workbook regularly – and remember to resave it when you make changes to it. If you haven't saved your workbook, and your computer crashes or you have a power failure, you may lose any unsaved data.

Save

Once the workbook has been saved you can save your changes to it whenever you wish.

◆ Click **Save**  on the Quick Access toolbar, or click the Microsoft Office button, then select **Save** to save any changes to it.

The Save As dialog box does not reappear, but the up-to-date version of your workbook replaces the old one saved to disk.

◆ Alternatively, press [Ctrl]-[S] to save your workbook.

Save vs Save As

There may be times when you save a workbook, edit it, then decide that you want to save the edited version of the workbook and keep the original version too. If you don't want to overwrite the original with the updated version, click the Microsoft Office Button and choose **Save As...** so you can select a different folder and/or filename for the new version of the file.

Password protection

If you wish to password protect your workbook (so that no one can open or edit the workbook unless they know the password) you can do so from the Save As dialog box.

1 Click **Tools** at the bottom left of the Save As dialog box.

2 Choose **General Options...**

3 Enter the password(s) and click **OK**.

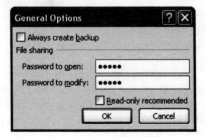

4 Re-enter the password(s) at the prompt.

5 Click **OK**.

Close workbook

♦ Click the Microsoft Office button, then click **Close**.

Or

♦ Click the **Close** button on the workbook title bar (if the workbook isn't maximized).

2.3 Moving around your worksheet

Before you can enter anything into a cell, you must make the cell you want to work on *active*. To make a single cell active, you must select it. You can easily move onto any cell (thus making it active) using either the keyboard or the mouse.

The active cell has a dark border. The address of the active cell appears in the Name box to the left of the formula bar.

Active cell

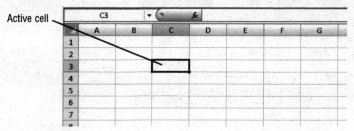

To make a cell active:

Using the mouse

♦ Click on the cell (you may need to use the horizontal or vertical scrollbars to bring it into view).

Using the keyboard

♦ Use the right, left, up and down arrow keys to move right or left one column, or up or down one row at a time.

♦ Hold down [Ctrl] and press an arrow key to move to the last occupied cell in that direction.

♦ Press [Enter] to move onto the cell directly below the one that is currently active.

You can also go to a specific cell, if you know its address.

To go to a specific cell:

♦ Type the cell address into the Name box and press [Enter].

Or

1 Press [F5].

2 Enter the address of the cell you want to go to in the **Reference** field of the **Go To** dialog box.

3 Click **OK**.

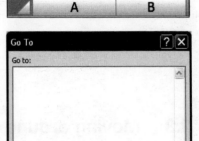

To return to cell A1 from anywhere in your worksheet:

♦ Hold down [Ctrl] and press [Home].

To move to the end of the work area on your worksheet (the last cell you have worked on, rather than cell XFD1048576):

♦ Hold down [Ctrl] and press [End].

Check out *Keyboard shortcuts* in the on-line Help to see if there are any others that you would find useful.

2.4   Selection techniques

You will often work on more than one cell at a time in Excel. You may need to format a group of cells in a particular way or copy or move a group, or apply a function to a group.

A group of cells is called a cell range. Ranges of adjacent cells are identified by the first cell address in the range, then a colon, followed by the last cell address, e.g. A1:A7, C3:D12; F5:H7. These ranges are highlighted below. Non-adjacent cell ranges have the cell addresses separated by commas.

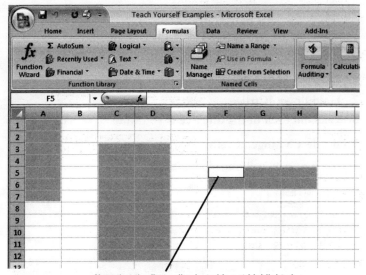

Note that the first cell selected is not highlighted

Using the mouse

To select a group of adjacent cells:

• Click and drag over the range of cells you wish to select.

Or

1 Click on a cell at one corner of the range you wish to select.
2 Hold down [Shift].
3 Click on the cell in the diagonally opposite corner of the range you want to select.

To select a row or rows:

• Click the number to the left of the row you want to select.

Or

• Drag down over the row numbers to select several rows.

To select a column or columns:

- Click the letter at the top of the column you want to select.

Or

- Drag across the column letters to select several columns.

To select the whole worksheet:

- Click the box at the far left of the column letters.

To select a range of non-adjacent cells:

1 Click on one of the cells you want to select.
2 Hold down [Ctrl].
3 Click on each of the other cells you want to select.

To deselect a range of cells:

- Click on any cell outside the range.

Select whole sheet   Select columns

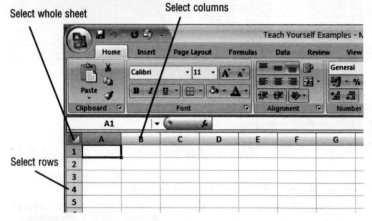

Select rows

Using the keyboard

To select a group of adjacent cells:

1 Click in a cell at the corner of the range you wish to select.
2 Hold down [Shift].
3 Press the arrow keys to move to the cell in the corner diagonally opposite, and release [Shift].

To deselect a range of cells:

- Press one of the arrow keys.

2.5 Entering text and numeric data

Each time you start Excel a new workbook is created. Entering text or data into your worksheet is easy.

1 Select the cell you want to enter text or data into.

2 Type in the text or data – the text or data will appear in the formula bar as well as in the active cell.

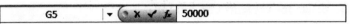

| G5 | ▼ | ⊗ ✗ ✓ ƒ× | 50000 |

3 Press [Enter] or click the 'tick' button to the left of the formula bar when you've completed the cell.

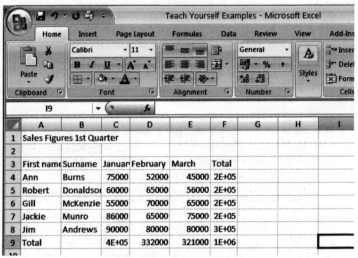

Things to note when entering numeric data:

◆ If a number won't fit in the cell, an *Exp* message or ###### is displayed.

◆ Numbers align by default to the right (see section 3.2).

Things to note when entering text:

◆ Text that doesn't fit into a single cell will 'spill over' into the cell to the right if that one is empty.

◆ Text that doesn't fit into a single cell will be only partially displayed if the cell to the right is not empty. You will need to widen the column (see section 2.7) to display all of the text.

◆ Text aligns by default to the left of a cell (see section 3.2).

2.6   Editing text and numeric data

If you make an error when entering data, you can fix things by:

- Deleting the contents of the cell.
- Replacing the contents of the cell.
- Editing the contents of the cell.

To delete the contents of a cell (or cells):

1   Select the cell (or cells) whose contents you want to erase.

2   Press [Delete].

Examples in this book

In this book we will use several worksheets to illustrate various features of Excel. I suggest you enter these examples into a workbook and use them as practice material. You can then follow the instructions and experiment with the features.

Simon's Sports

The first worksheet will display a list of items that are in a sale in Simon's Sports. Enter the text displayed in the worksheet below and build up the worksheet as you work through the rest of the chapter.

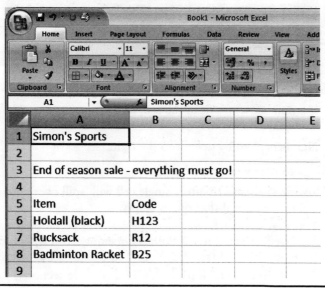

To replace all the contents of a cell:

1 Select the cell whose contents you want to replace.

2 Type in the text or data that should be in the cell.

To edit the contents of a cell:

1 Select the cell whose contents you want to edit.

2 Click in the Formula bar.

3 Edit the cell contents as required (move right and left using the arrow keys, delete characters using [**Delete**] or [**Backspace**], or enter text or data through the keyboard).

4 Press [**Enter**] when you've finished editing to return to the worksheet.

Or

1 Double-click in the cell whose contents you want to edit – this places the insertion point within the cell.

2 Edit the cell contents as required.

3 Press [**Enter**] when you've finished editing.

2.7 Column width

If the text you are entering into a cell is more than the column width will accommodate, you must do something about it if you want it to be fully visible.

Sometimes – particularly with main headings at the top of a worksheet – it doesn't matter if the text spills over into the cells to the right. However, when entering column headings or row labels each entry should occupy a single cell – with no overspill into the next column.

One way to make text fit into a single cell is to adjust the width of the column.

Manual adjustment

To change the width of a column:

◆ In the column heading row, click and drag the vertical line to the right of the column whose width you want to change – in this example we need to widen column A.

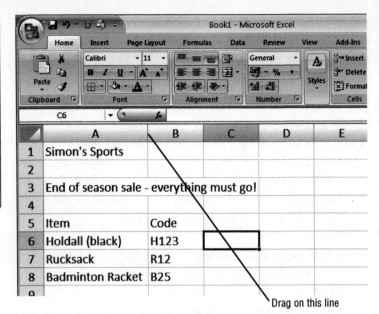

Drag on this line

To set a column to a specific width:

1 Select any cell in the column you want to adjust.

2 Display the **Home** tab on the Ribbon.

3 Click the **Format** button on the **Cells** group.

4 Select **Width…**

5 Complete the **Column Width** dialog box – the value is the number of characters that will fit in the standard font.

6 Click **OK**.

To change the column width to fit the contents:

1 Select the cell that will determine the width of your column.

2 Click the **Format** button on the **Cells** group.

3 Choose **AutoFit Selection**.

- You can quickly format all column widths to automatically fit – click the **Select All** button – then double-click any boundary between the column headings.

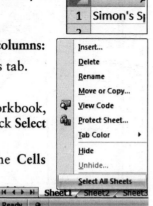

Select All

1 Simon's S

Insert...
Delete
Rename
Move or Copy...
View Code
Protect Sheet...
Tab Color ▶
Hide
Unhide...
Select All Sheets

To change the default width for all columns:

1 Select the worksheet – click on its tab.

Or

- To set the default for the whole workbook, – right-click on a sheet tab and click **Select All Sheets**.

2 Click the **Format** button on the **Cells** group.

3 Select **Standard Width...**

4 Enter the width required and click **OK**.

AutoFit

You can get Excel to automatically adjust the width of the column to fit the entries within it.

To adjust the column width automatically:

- In the column heading row, double-click the vertical line to the right of the column you want to adjust.

2.8 Other text cell formatting options
Wrap text

To specify that text should wrap within a cell:

1 Select the cells you want to set the text wrap option for.

Alignment

2 On the **Home** tab, click the **Wrap text** tool in the **Alignment** group.

You will find other options in the Format Cells dialog box.

- To open the dialog box, click the **Format** button in the **Cells** group, and choose **Format Cells...** from the options.

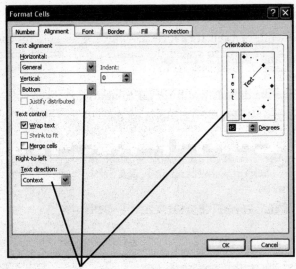

Experiment with other options to see what effect they have

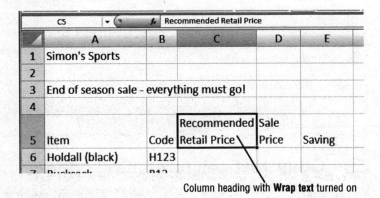

Column heading with **Wrap text** turned on

Text rotation

To rotate text within a cell:

1 Select the cell(s).

2 Click the **Orientation** tool in the **Alignment** group on the **Home** tab.

3 Select a text orientation from the options.

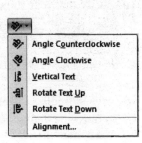

Shrink to Fit

If the contents of a cell are a little too wide for the column width, and you don't want to widen the column, you can get the contents of the cell to 'shrink to fit'.

1 Select the cell whose contents you want to shrink to fit.

2 Click the **Format** button in the **Cells** group on the **Home** tab, and select **Format Cells...** from the options.

3 On the **Alignment** tab, select the **Shrink to fit** checkbox and click **OK**.

2.9 Number formats

Much of the data entered into worksheets is currency. Most of the time that you have a currency value, you will want the appropriate currency symbol to precede the value – the £, • or other currency symbol.

To place a currency symbol in front of a figure:

◆ Format the cells to display the entry in a currency format.

Or

◆ Enter the symbol through the keyboard.

If you enter your figures through the numeric keypad, it's probably easiest to format the cells to display the figures as currency.

You can format cells *before* or *after* you have entered your text or data.

To format the cells to display the figures in currency format:

1 Select the cells you want to format (see section 2.4 above)

2 Click the currency button in the **Number** group on the **Home** tab if you want the £ symbol, or click the drop-down arrow on this button and select the symbol required.

The Number group has some other buttons to help you format numbers – Percent style, Comma style, Increase and Decrease decimal (these two change the number of decimal places displayed). Other number formats can be found on the **Number** tab in the **Format Cells** dialog box – have a look to see if any would be useful.

To apply a format from the Format Cells dialog box:

1 Select the cells you want to format.

2 Click the **Format** button in the **Cells** group then click **Format Cells...**

3 Select the Number tab in the Format Cells dialog box.

4 Choose a category from the list.

5 Complete the dialog box as required – exactly what appears in it depends on the category you select.

6 Click **OK**.

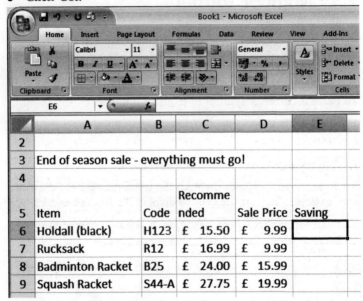

2.10 Formulas

Any cell in your workbook, which will contain a figure that has been calculated using other entries in your workbook, should have a formula or function in it (do *not* do your calculations on a calculator, then type the answer into your workbook).

Formulas allow you to add, subtract, multiply, divide and work out percentages of the values in cells.

Operators used in formulas are:

+	Add	-	Subtract
/	Divide	*	Multiply
%	Percentage		

In our example we are going to use a formula to work out how much a customer will save if they buy something out of the sale.

To work out the saving for the first item in the list (the holdall), we need to subtract the sale price (the figure in cell D6) from the recommended retail price (in cell C6). The result of this calculation should be displayed in cell E6, in the *Saving* column.

To enter the formula:

1 Select the cell that will contain the result of the calculation (E6 in this example).

2 Press the [=] key on your keyboard (to tell Excel we're entering a formula).

3 Click on cell C6 (the retail price cell for the item).

• The cell address appears in the formula bar *and* in the current cell.

4 Press the [-] key on your keyboard (we're subtracting).

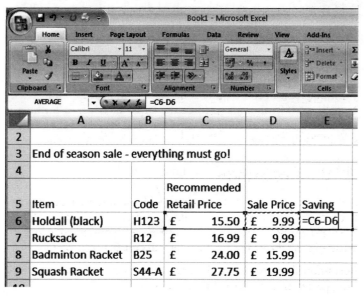

5 Click on cell D6 (the cell containing the *sale price* figure).

6 Press [Enter]. The result will appear in cell E6.

At step 3 and step 5, I suggested you click on the cell you want to use in a formula. If you prefer, you can enter the cell address manually by typing the coordinates into your formula instead.

Simple formula examples

=A7/B6   Divide the figure in A7 by the figure in B6

=D22*12   Multiply the figure in D22 by 12

=C7*25%   Calculate 25% of the figure in C7

Order of precedence

If there is a mixture of operators in a formula, Excel will deal with the multiplication and division *before* it deals with the addition and subtraction.

   =A4+C7*D7

Multiply the figure in C7 by the one in D7, and add the answer to the figure in A4.

   =A1+B2/C3+D4*E5-F2

Add to the figure in A1, the result of dividing the figure in B2 by that in C3, then add the result of multiplying the figure in D4 by that in E5, then subtract the figure in F2.

Parentheses

Formulas can become quite long and complicated – and tricky to follow! If you want to force the order in which a formula is calculated, or make a long one easier to read, use parentheses ( ). In the example below, the calculation in each set of parentheses is solved *before* working through the formula – and the result is different from the formula without parentheses.

   =(A1+B2)/C3+(D4*(E5-F2))

Add A1 to B2   we'll call this XX

Subtract F2 from E5   we'll call this YY

Multiply YY by D4   we'll call this ZZ

To get the final result:
Divide XX by C3 then add ZZ.

To help you remember this, think BODMAS! Brackets first, then Division and Multiplication, and then Addition and Subtraction. *Always* work left to right and *never* move the position of the entries you are calculating.

2.11 AutoFill

In Simon's Sports sale worksheet, we could work down the column entering the formula for each *Saving* cell as described in section 2.10. However, a much quicker way to achieve the same result is to use AutoFill. This allows you to *copy* a formula from one cell into adjacent cells – to the right, left, up or down.

To AutoFill the formula in E6 to the other Saving cells:

1 Select E6.

2 Position the pointer over the bottom right corner of the cell – the Fill Handle (a small black cross) should appear.

3 Click and drag the cross down over the other *Saving* cells.

When you release the mouse, the formula in cell E6 will be copied to the cells you dragged over.

	A	B	C	D	E
2					
3	End of season sale - everything must go!				
4					
5	Item	Code	Recommended Retail Price	Sale Price	Saving
6	Holdall (black)	H123	£ 15.50	£ 9.99	£ 5.51
7	Rucksack	R12	£ 16.99	£ 9.99	
8	Badminton Racket	B25	£ 24.00	£ 15.99	
9	Squash Racket	S44-A	£ 27.75	£ 19.99	
10					
11					

If you click on each cell in the saving column and keep an eye on the Formula bar, you will notice that Excel has automatically changed the cell addresses in the formula *relative* to the position you have copied the formula to. Neat trick!

When you AutoFill text or data, a Smart tag appears below the data that you have copied. Click the Smart tag to see the AutoFill options. If you don't want the default, click the option required.

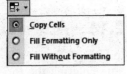

○	Copy Cells
○	Fill Formatting Only
○	Fill Without Formatting

• Once a formula has been copied into cell, as in column E in this example, it will extend down the column automatically as you add new rows! If you type in another item in row 10, the formula in row 9 will copy to row 10 once the required data is entered. Add this data and watch what happens!

Hockey Stick	H220	£ 16.99	£ 9.99
Rucksack	R15	£ 40.00	£ 29.99
Hockey Stick	H221	£ 18.99	£ 10.99
Dumbell Set	D12	£ 36.99	£ 24.00
Home Gym	HG3	£ 245.99	£ 175.00
Tennis Racket	T101	£ 36.99	£ 25.99
Rucksack	R10	£ 7.99	£ 5.49

AutoFill can be a real time-saver in some situations. Try this:

To enter column or row labels for each month of the year or day of the week:

1 Enter the first month or day you want to use into the appropriate cell – January or Jan, September or Sept, Wednesday or Wed.

2 AutoFill the contents of that cell across the columns or down the rows.

• Excel will automatically complete the other cells.

To enter a row or column of numbers in sequence, e.g. 1, 2, 3, 4 etc. or 50, 100, 150 etc.:

1 Enter the first two numbers in two adjacent cells.

2 Select both cells.

3 AutoFill down the rows or across the columns.

If you want to enter dates, you can use the Fill option. The date can be incremented using every day of the week (day), weekdays only (Monday to Friday), months or years.

1 Enter the first date in your series.

2 Click and drag the **Fill Handle** using the *right* mouse button.

3 When you release, a pop-up menu appears.

4 Select the fill option you require – **Fill Days, Fill Weekdays, Fill Months** or **Fill Years**.

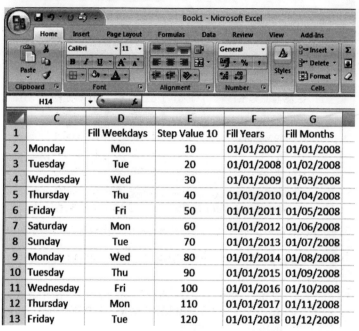

	C	D	E	F	G
1		Fill Weekdays	Step Value 10	Fill Years	Fill Months
2	Monday	Mon	10	01/01/2007	01/01/2008
3	Tuesday	Tue	20	01/01/2008	01/02/2008
4	Wednesday	Wed	30	01/01/2009	01/03/2008
5	Thursday	Thu	40	01/01/2010	01/04/2008
6	Friday	Fri	50	01/01/2011	01/05/2008
7	Saturday	Mon	60	01/01/2012	01/06/2008
8	Sunday	Tue	70	01/01/2013	01/07/2008
9	Monday	Wed	80	01/01/2014	01/08/2008
10	Tuesday	Thu	90	01/01/2015	01/09/2008
11	Wednesday	Fri	100	01/01/2016	01/10/2008
12	Thursday	Mon	110	01/01/2017	01/11/2008
13	Friday	Tue	120	01/01/2018	01/12/2008

Examples of some of the Fill options are displayed above.

♦ Columns C and D show different day formats AutoFilled.

♦ Column E shows figures with an increment of 10 AutoFilled.

♦ Column F has been completed using the Fill Years option on the pop-up menu.

♦ Column G has been completed using the Fill Months option on the pop-up menu.

2.12 Another worksheet!

Use this example to get some more practice. Enter the text and data below into a different worksheet in your workbook. To select a different worksheet, click the sheet tab – Sheet1, Sheet2, Sheet 3, etc. to the left of the horizontal scroll bar. It doesn't matter what sheet you use. This example is for a stock value table for *Screw the Nut plc*. Use the following notes to help you get the layout and formulas correct.

	A	B	C	D	E	F	G
1	SCREW THE NUT PLC						
2							
3	Stock Value Data						
4							
5	Part No	Description	Cost (trade)	Cost (retail)	Profit	Number in Stock	Value of Stock
6	S113	Screwdriver Set	£ 10.00	£ 18.99	£ 8.99	4	£ 40.00
7	S2451	Spanner set	£ 14.00	£ 20.99	£ 6.99	6	£ 84.00
8	W2201	Wrench and Grip set	£ 9.00	£ 15.99	£ 6.99	6	£ 54.00
9	W3120	Workman (B&D)	£ 60.00	£ 75.00	£ 15.00	3	£180.00
10							
11						Total value of stock	£358.00

- Enter the titles and column headings, *Part No*, *Description*, *Cost (trade)*, *Cost (retail)*, *Profit* and *Number in Stock*.

- Format row 5 to allow text wrap in the cells (see section 2.8).

- Format the data cells in the *Cost (trade)*, *Cost (retail)*, *Profit* and *Value of Stock* columns to display the figures as currency (see section 2.9).

- Enter a formula to calculate the *Profit* figure. For the first item (screwdriver set) it would be =D6-C6 (see section 2.10 for information on entering formulas).

- The *Number in Stock* figures are centred in this example (see section 3.2 for more on alignment).

- Enter a formula to calculate the *Value of Stock* column. For the first item it would be =C6*F6 (if you base the stock value on the trade price).

- AutoFill the formulas down the columns (see section 2.11).

- The *Total value of Stock* figure could be calculated by entering the formula =G6+G7+G8+G9 (you could also use the AutoSum function for this – see section 5.1).

2.13 Move or copy cell contents

If you enter text or data into your worksheet, and it's correct, but in the wrong place you can move it to where it should be (rather than delete it and re-type it in the correct location).

To move the contents of cells:

Cut and Paste

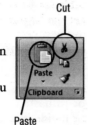

1 Select the cells you want to move.

2 Click the **Cut** tool in the **Clipboard** group on the Home tab.

3 Select the top leftmost cell of the range you want to move the text or data to.

4 Click the **Paste** tool in the **Clipboard** group.

Or

Drag and Drop

1 Select the cells you want to move.

2 Point to the edge of the selected area – the mouse pointer displays four directional arrows.

3 Drag and drop the cells into the new position.

To copy the contents of cells:

Copy and Paste

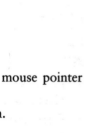

1 Select the cells you want to copy.

2 Click the **Copy** tool in the **Clipboard** group.

♦ A dotted line appears around the cells.

3 Select the top left cell of the range to copy the data to.

4 Click the **Paste** tool in the **Clipboard** group.

♦ If you want more than one copy, repeat steps 3 and 4 until you have all the copies required.

♦ When you paste, a SmartTag appears below the data. Click this to display the paste options and select one if you do not want the default.

5 Press [Esc] to cancel the dotted line around the copied cells.

Or Drag and Drop

1 Select the cells you want to copy.

2 Point to the edge of the selected area – the mouse pointer displays four directional arrows.

3 Hold down [Ctrl] (the pointer changes to a white arrow with + beside it) while you drag and drop the cells. Release the mouse button *before* [Ctrl] – if you don't, you'll move the cells instead of copying them.

Paste Special

Paste Special allows you to be selective about what you paste – the functions, formatting, comments, etc. – or to paste data and add, subtract, multiply or divide it into existing data.

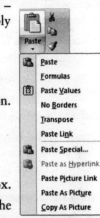

1 Copy or cut the data.

2 Select the cell(s) to paste the data into.

3 Click the arrow beneath the **Paste** button.

4 Select an option from the list.

Or

Click **Paste Special...**

5 Select what to paste from the dialog box.

6 Choose the operation to perform with the pasted data (if any).

7 Click **OK**.

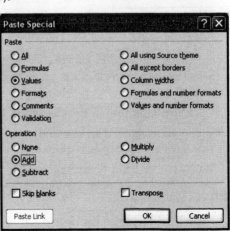

2.14   Insert/delete rows and columns

As you build up your worksheet, you may discover that you have added a row or column that you don't require, or have perhaps missed out a row or column that you do need.

To insert a row:

1   Select the row (see section 2.4) that will go *below* the row you are inserting.

2   Right-click within the selected area and choose **Insert** from the pop-up menu.

To insert a column:

1   Select the column (see section 2.4) that will go to the right of the column you are inserting.

2   Right-click within the selected area and choose **Insert**.

To delete a row or column:

1   Select the row or column (see section 2.4) you wish to delete.

2   Right-click within the selected area and choose **Delete**.

To add or delete several rows or columns at the same time:

1   Click and drag in the row or column label area to indicate how many rows or columns you want to insert or delete.

2   Right-click in the selected area and choose **Insert** or **Delete**.

2.15   View options

The way your worksheet appears on the screen is influenced by the view options you have selected. There are many options that can change the way your worksheet looks. We will consider some of the more commonly used ones here – others will be introduced as appropriate throughout the book.

Zoom

The Zoom affects the size of your worksheet on the screen. The default zoom is 100%, but you can increase this to make your worksheet easier to read, or decrease it so you can see more information on the screen at one time.

To change the zoom option:

- Click the increase (plus) and decrease (minus) buttons at the bottom right of the status bar.

Normal, Page Layout and Page Break views

Most people work in Normal view when developing their worksheets. Other regularly-used views are:

- **Page Layout** – which shows the margin area and header and footer areas of a page as well as the print area.
- **Page Break Preview** – which shows you where the page breaks will be if you print your worksheet.

There are tools for each of these views to the left of the zoom area on the Status bar.

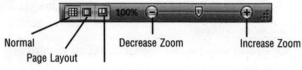

Normal

Page Layout

Page Break Preview

Decrease Zoom

Increase Zoom

View tab

You will also find view options on the View tab in the Ribbon. The Workbook View group contains Normal, Page Layout and Page Break Preview command buttons and the Zoom group has additional zoom options.

2.16   Print Preview and Print

At some stage you will want to print your file. Before printing, it's a good idea to *preview* it. It takes practice to get a good fit, and previewing gives you the chance to see how the sheet will look when printed. You can then adjust settings before printing. Page layout options are discussed in section 3.9.

Print Preview

To preview your worksheet:

- Click the Microsoft Office button, then click the arrow next to **Print**, and select **Print Preview**.

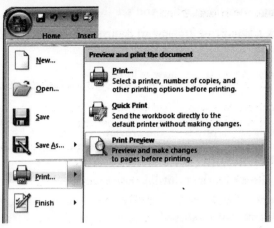

A preview of the current worksheet will be displayed on your screen, in full-page view. It doesn't matter if you can't read what is on the screen – the preview is there to let you see how your worksheet will fit onto your paper. You get an idea of how well the data, white space, graphics, etc. will look on the page.

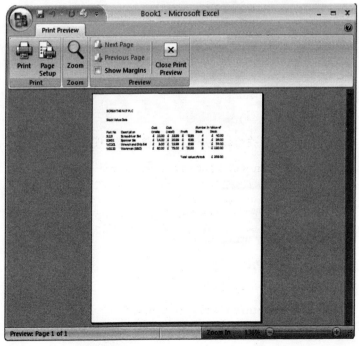

To change something when you see the preview:

1 Click **Close Print Preview** to return to your worksheet.

2 Edit the worksheet as required.

3 Preview again to see how it looks.

Print

When you are happy with the preview, you can send it to print.

To print from Print Preview:

1 Click **Print** on the Print Preview Ribbon.

2 Complete the **Print** dialog box – set **Number of copies** and **Print range** as required.

3 Click **OK**.

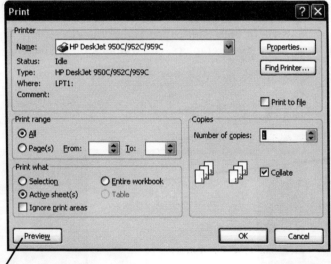

You can preview from the Print dialog box

To print one copy using the default settings:

◆ Click **Quick Print** on the **Print** area of the Microsoft Office button menu.

To select print options:

1 Click the Microsoft Office button and select **Print**.

2 Specify the options in the **Print** dialog box and click **OK**.

To print part of your worksheet:

If you don't want to print all of your worksheet, you can print the area required on its own.

1 Select the range of cells you want to print.

2 Open the **File** menu and choose **Print...**

3 Select **Selection** from the **Print what** options.

4 Click **OK**.

Summary

In this chapter we have discussed some of the basic skills required when using Excel.

- Spreadsheet jargon
- Cell names and ranges
- File handling – Save, Close, Open and New
- Moving around a worksheet
- Selection techniques – for rows, columns, adjacent and non-adjacent cells
- Entering text and numeric data
- Deleting, replacing and editing the contents of a cell
- Adjusting column widths
- Wrapping text within a cell and 'shrink to fit'
- Number formats
- Entering simple formulas
- Order of precedence and the use of parentheses
- AutoFill
- Moving and copying cells
- Inserting and deleting rows and columns
- Print Preview and Print.

03 formatting and layout

In this chapter you will learn:

- some more formatting options
- how to freeze panes
- how to split the screen
- how to set page layout options

3.1 Font group

The most commonly used Font formatting options are located in the Font group on the Home tab.

Some of the buttons are toggles, e.g. Bold, Italic and Underline – click to select or deselect the format. Others, e.g. Font, Font Size, Border, Cell Fill Colour and Font Colour – have drop-down arrows that display their options.

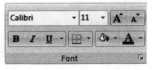

* To access the **Font** tab in the **Format Cells** dialog box, click the **Format Cells** dialog box launcher button at the bottom right corner of the **Font** group. This tab has a few more formatting options than are found in the Font group.

Bold, italic and underline

To apply/remove bold, italic or single underline formatting:

1 Select the cell(s) you wish to format.

2 Click **B** or **I** or **U** to apply or remove the format.

3 Deselect the cell(s).

The keyboard shortcuts for these are:

* [Ctrl]-[B] for **bold**
* [Ctrl]-[I] for *italics*
* [Ctrl]-[U] for <u>underline</u>.

To apply double underline, click the drop-down arrow to the right of the underline button, and select **Double Underline**.

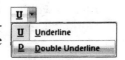

Font and font size

The default font used in Excel is Calibri, the default font size is 11. You can use the Font or Font Size command button to change these settings if you wish.

To change the font or font size:

1 Select the cell(s) you wish to change the formatting for.

2 Click the arrow to the right of the Font or Font Size button.

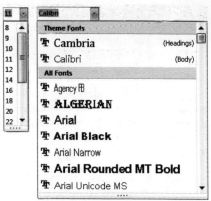

3 Select the font or size – if you hover over an option you will get a live preview of that option in the selected cell(s)

4 Deselect the cell(s).

◆ The **Increase Font Size** and **Decrease Font Size** buttons can be used to change the font size. Select the cell(s), then click the **Increase** or **Decrease Font Size** button to set the size.

◆ You can type the name or size into the **Font** or **Font Size** field and press [**Enter**] to change the font or size.

To change the default font:

1 Click the Microsoft Office button and choose **Excel Options**.

2 Select **Popular** from the list of options on the left.

3 Specify the font you wish to use in the **Use this font**: field.

4 Set the default font size in the **Font size** field.

5 Click **OK**.

◆ You will need to restart Excel for your settings to take effect. All new workbooks will be affected by this change – existing workbooks will not be affected.

Live Preview

This can be switched on or off in the Excel Options dialog box.

1 Click the Microsoft Office button and choose **Excel Options**.

2 In the **Popular** options, select or deselect **Enable Live Preview** as required.

3 Click **OK**.

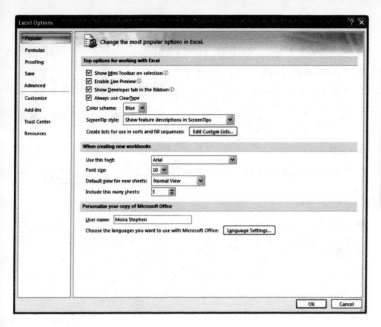

Font colour

To change the colour of the font:

1 Select the cell(s).

2 Click the arrow to the right of the **Font Color** button.

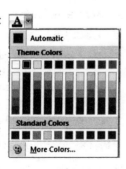

* The font colour of the selected cell(s) changes automatically as you move the pointer over the colours.

3 Select the colour required.

* Click **More Colors...** to access the **Color** dialog box and even more colours.

4 Deselect the cell(s).

* If you display a list of options, e.g. the font or colour and then decide that you do not want to choose anything, just click anywhere on your worksheet to cancel the procedure.

Fill Colour

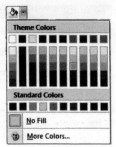

To change the fill colour of your cell(s):

1 Select the cell(s).

2 Click the arrow to the right of the **Fill Color** button.

3 Select the colour required.

4 Deselect your cell(s).

♦ You will find more fill options, e.g. fill effects and pattern options, on the **Fill** tab in the **Format Cells** dialog box.

Borders

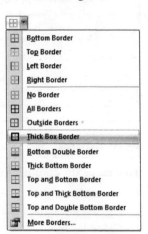

To apply borders to your cells:

1 Select the cell(s).

2 Click the arrow to the right of the **Border** button.

3 Select the border option required.

Or

4 Click **More Borders...** to display the **Borders** tab of the **Format Cells** dialog box for more options.

3.2 Alignment group

When you enter data into your cells, the default horizontal alignment is left for text, and right for numbers. The default vertical alignment or text and numbers is at the bottom.

The **Alignment** group on the **Home** tab has a variety of alignment options to choose from.

To align data horizontally within a cell:

1 Select the cell(s) you wish to format.

2 Click the **Align Left**, **Center** or **Align Right** button.

3 Deselect the cell(s).

To align a cell entry with the top, middle or bottom of a cell:

1 Select the cell(s) you wish to format.

2 Click the **Top, Middle** or **Bottom Align** button.

3 Deselect the cell(s).

To change the orientation of a cell entry

The orientation of a cell entry is often adjusted when labelling narrow columns.

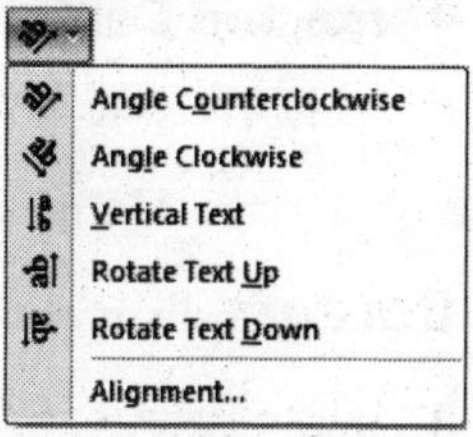

| Angle Counterclockwise |
| Angle Clockwise |
| Vertical Text |
| Rotate Text Up |
| Rotate Text Down |
| Alignment... |

1 Select the cell(s).

2 Click the arrow beside the **Orientation** button.

3 Select the option required.

4 Deselect the cell(s).

Some of the alignment options are displayed here:

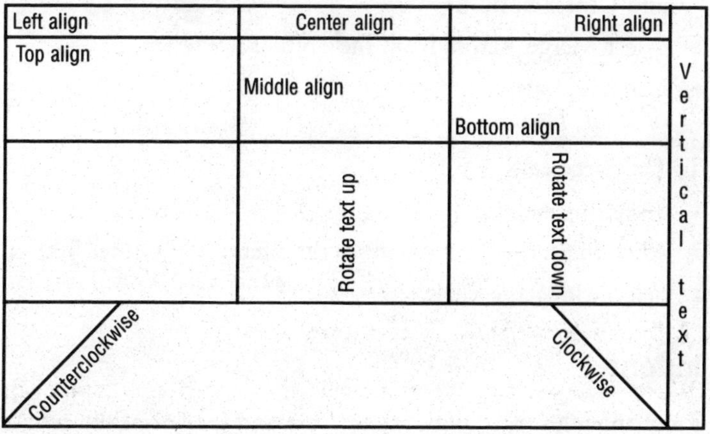

Left align	Center align	Right align	
Top align	Middle align	Bottom align	V e r t i c a l
	Rotate text up	Rotate text down	t e x t
Counterclockwise		Clockwise	

Wrap text

If you want text to display in one cell, rather than adjust the width of the cell if the text doesn't fit, you can wrap it within the cell. The row height will then adjust to accommodate the entry.

1 Select the cell(s) you wish to format.

2 Click the **Wrap text** command button.

3 Deselect the cell(s).

Merge Cells

Worksheet headings (rather than column headings) often run across several columns. You can easily merge the cells in the heading row to improve the layout of your worksheet.

- Ensure that the text you wish displayed in the merged cell is in the top left-most cell of those to be merged. Any data not in the top left-most cell is lost as a result of the merge.

Merge and Center

1 Select the cells you wish to merge.

2 Click the **Merge and Center** button ⊞.

To **merge cells without centring the data:**

1 Select the cells you wish to merge.

2 Click the arrow to the right of the **Merge and Center** button.

3 Select **Merge Across** from the options.

| Merge and Center |
| Merge Across |
| Merge Cells |
| UnMerge Cells |

- You could also use the **Merge Cells** option for this.

To **UnMerge cells:**

1 Select the cell.

2 Click the arrow to the right of the Merge and Center button.

3 Select **UnMerge Cells**.

Indent

To **change the space between the text and the left of the cell:**

1 Select the cell(s).

2 Click the **Increase Indent** or **Decrease Indent** button until you have the effect you want.

- To access the **Alignment** tab in the **Format Cells** dialog box, click the **Alignment** dialog box launcher button at the bottom right of the Alignment group.

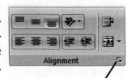

Alignment dialog box launcher

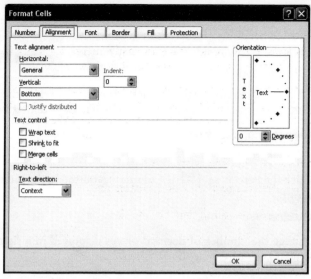

Use the Alignment tab to set several aspects of alignment at the same time.

3.3 Number formats

Many of the cells in a worksheet will contain numeric data – monetary figures, percentages, integers, etc. The most commonly used number formats are in the **Number** group on the **Home** tab.

The **Category** field shows the category of the selected cell.

To change the category:

◆ Click the drop-down arrow and select the category from the list.

To format cells as currency – £:

1 Select the cell(s).

2 Click the **Currency** button in the **Number** group.

To format cells as currency – euro or dollar:

1 Select the cell(s).

2 Click the arrow beside the **Currency** button.

3 Select an option.

* To use a different currency, click **More...** and select the options from the **Number** tab in the **Format Cells** dialog box.

To format using the Percent style or Comma style:

1 Select the cell(s).

2 Click the **Percentage** 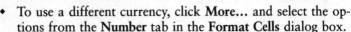 or **Comma** button in the **Number** group.

3 Deselect your cell(s).

To change the number of decimal places displayed in a figure:

1 Select the cell(s).

2 Click the **Increase** or **Decrease Decimal** button.

3 Deselect your cell(s).

Additional number formatting options can be found on the **Number** tab in the **Format Cells** dialog box – click the **Format Cells** dialog box launcher button at the bottom right of the **Number** group.

3.4 Format Painter

If you have applied several formatting options to a cell, and you want to apply the same formatting to some other cells in your worksheet you could save yourself some time by using the Format Painter.

The Format Painter allows you to copy the formatting from one cell, and paint it on to other cells.

To copy a format to a single cell, or to adjacent cells:

1 Select the cell that is formatted the way you want.

2 Click the **Format Painter** button in the **Clipboard** group on the **Home** tab.

3 Click on the cell to apply the formatting.

Or

• Click and drag over the cells to apply the formatting.

To copy a format to non-adjacent cells:

1 Select the cell that is formatted the way you want.

2 Double-click the **Format Painter** button – this 'locks' the Format Painter tool on.

3 Click on each cell to apply the formatting.

Or

1 Drag over the cells you want to paint with the formatting.

2 Click the **Format Painter** button again (or press [**Esc**]) to switch the Format Painter off when you've finished.

3.5 Standard styles

A style is a set of formatting options that you save as a group. When you want to apply the formats held in a style, you apply the style, rather than each of the options individually.

If you don't apply a style to text or data, it is formatted using the Normal style.

If you format data using the Currency, Comma Style or Percent Style buttons in the Number group you are applying a predefined style. Other predefined styles in the Cell Styles list are: Currency (0 decimal places) and Comma (0 decimal places).

Using styles has two main benefits:

• **Consistency** – when you apply a style, all the formatting options contained within it are applied in one go (you won't accidentally use the wrong font size or colour).

• **Speed** – it's usually quicker to apply a style than to apply several options individually using the command buttons.

You can apply a style to an individual cell, or a group of cells.

1 Select the cell(s) you wish to apply a style to.

2 Click **Cell Styles** in the **Cells** group on the **Home** tab.

3 Select the style required.

Good, Bad and Neutral				
Normal	Bad	Good	Neutral	

Data and Model

Calculation	Check Cell	Input	Linked Cell	Note
Output	Warning Text			

Titles and Headings

Headin...	Heading 2	Heading 3	Heading 4	Sheet ...
Total				

Themed Cell Styles

Accent1	Accent1 - 2...	Accent1 - 4...	Accent1 - 6...	Accent2
Accent2 - 2...	Accent2 - 4...	Accent2 - 6...	Accent3	Accent3 - 2...
Accent3 - 4...	Accent3 - 6...	Accent4	Accent4 - 2...	Accent4 - 4...
Accent4 - 6...	Accent5	Accent5 - 2...	Accent5 - 4...	Accent5 - 6...
Accent6	Accent6 - 2...	Accent6 - 4...	Accent6 - 6...	Emphasis 1
Emphasis 2	Emphasis 3			

Number Format

Comma	Comma [0]	Currency	Currency [0]	Percent

New Cell Style...

Merge Styles

• Note that the **Cell Styles** also has Number formats.

Apply some styles to your Simon's Sports worksheet. Use the Titles and Headings styles, or the Themed Cell Styles, e.g.:

• Heading 1 to the 'Simon's Sports' heading,

• Heading 2 to the 'End of Season Sale – Everything must go!!'

• Heading 3 to the column headings in the Simon's Sports worksheet.

We will discuss creating your own styles in Chapter 8.

3.6 Conditional formatting

Conditional formatting is used to format a cell (or range of cells), if specific conditions are met. It's useful if you want to be able to highlight cells that contain values that are higher or lower than you would expect, or within a certain range. By applying conditional formatting you can identify such data at a glance. For example, you may have a list of figures, and want all those that are >=50000 (more than or equal to) displayed in red and italics, and all those figures that are <50000 (less than) in green.

+ When creating a conditional format you can reference other cells in the same worksheet e.g. = FA5000, but you cannot use references to an external workbook.

To apply a conditional format:

1 Select the cells that you want to apply the formatting to.

2 Click the **Conditional Formatting** button in the **Styles** group on the **Home** tab.

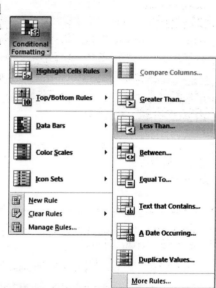

3 Select **Highlight Cells Rules**.

4 Select the rule.

5 Complete the dialog box with details of your new rule.

6 Click **OK**.

7 Repeat steps 1–6 for each rule you want applied to the cells.

If you wish to create a new rule for high-lighting cells, select the **More Rules...** option at the bottom of the **Highlight Cells Rules** list, and complete the dialog box with details of the rule you wish to set up.

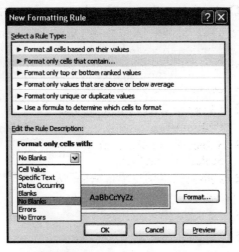

To delete rules:

1 Select the cells that have rules applied (if necessary).

2 Click the **Conditional Formatting** button.

3 Select **Clear Rules**.

4 Click on **Selected Cells** or **Entire Sheet**, depending on where you wish to remove the rules from.

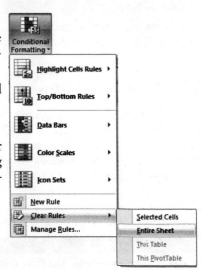

Top/Bottom Rules

This allows you to quickly format the specified top or bottom:

* number of items,
* percentage of items, or
* those above or below average.

Data Bars, Color Scales and Icon Sets

You can quickly add a Data Bar, Color Scale or Icon Set formatting option to a range of scales using the preset formats available, or by customizing these to suit your requirements.

1 Select the cells to format.

2 Click the **Conditional Formatting** button.

3 Select **Data Bars** or **Color Scales** or **Icon Sets**.

4 Choose the one you wish to use.

5 Click **Preview** to see the effect.

6 Repeat 4 and 5 as necessary.

7 Click **OK**.

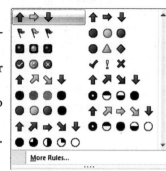

♦ To customize any of the settings, or set up another rule, click **More Rules...** and complete the dialog box as required.

3.7 Freeze panes

Many of the worksheets you create will be considerably larger than will fit on to your computer screen. You will need to scroll vertically and horizontally to display the data you want to work with. When you scroll your worksheet, the column headings or row labels will disappear off your screen as the other data appears. This is often inconvenient, as you need to see the headings and labels to make sense of your data. In these situations you should *freeze* the heading columns and rows so that they stay in place and only the data cells scroll.

To freeze the top row or the first column:

1 Select the **View** tab on the Ribbon.

2 Click the **Freeze Panes** button in the **Window** group.

3 Select **Freeze Top Row** or **Freeze First Column**.

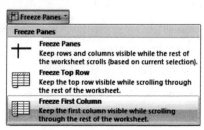

To freeze a row (or rows):

1 Select the row below the ones you want to freeze.

Or

To freeze a column (or columns):

◆ Select the column to the right of the ones you want to freeze.

Or

To freeze both a row (or rows) and column (or columns):

◆ Select the cell below and to the right of where you want to freeze the panes.

2 Open the **Window** menu.

3 Choose **Freeze Panes**.

The worksheet will be divided into separate panes.

When you scroll through your worksheet horizontally, the column or columns you have frozen remain in view. When you scroll through your worksheet vertically the row or rows you have frozen will remain in view when the other data scrolls.

The heavy line indicates the edge of the frozen pane
Rows 1–4 are frozen

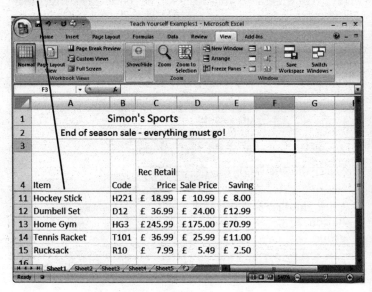

To unfreeze panes:

1 Click the **Freeze Panes** command button.

2 Choose **Unfreeze Panes**.

3.8 Split screen

There will also be times when you want to compare the data on one part of your worksheet with that on another – but the data ranges that you want to compare are in separate areas of the worksheet. When this happens, you should *split* your screen so that you can scroll each part independently, to bring the data you require into view.

Split box

If you look carefully above the top of the vertical scroll bar or just to the right of the horizontal scroll bar, you will notice the *split boxes*. Use these to split your screen.

To split your screen horizontally:

♦ Drag the split box at the top of the vertical scroll bar down to where you want your split to be.

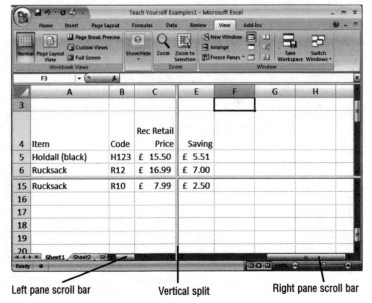

Left pane scroll bar   Vertical split   Right pane scroll bar

To split your screen vertically:

◆ Drag the split box at the right of the horizontal scroll bar along to where you want your split to be.

When your screen is split, you can scroll each pane independently to view the data you want to see.

To remove a split:

◆ Double-click on the split.

3.9 Page setup

In Chapter 2 we discussed printing. We will now consider some ways in which you can change the appearance (or layout) of the printed sheet.

Margins

The margin is the amount of white space between the edge of the paper and where your worksheet area starts.

The normal margin settings are:

◆ Top and Bottom – 1.91 cm

◆ Right and left – 1.78 cm

◆ Header and footer – 0.76 cm.

To change these margins:

1 Select the **Page Layout** tab on the Ribbon.

2 Click the **Margins** button in the **Page Setup** group.

3 Choose **Wide** or **Narrow** margins.

Or

4 Click **Custom Margins…** to display the dialog box, where you can specify the exact measurements you require.

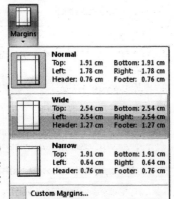

Orientation

Pages are usually printed portrait (rather than landscape), and on A4 paper.

To change the orientation:

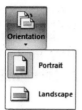

1 Select the **Page Layout** tab.

2 Click the **Orientation** button in the **Page Setup** group.

3 Choose the orientation.

Paper Size

The default paper size is Letter.

1 Click the **Size** button in the **Page Setup** group on the **Page Layout** tab.

2 Select the paper size required from the list.

Or

3 Click **More...** and select the size from the dialog box.

Print Area

If you regularly print part of your worksheet, you can specify the range as a print area. This is the area that Excel will then print as the default. A print area remains set until you clear it.

To set the print area:

1 Select the range of cells.

2 Go to the **Page Setup** group on the **Page Layout** tab.

3 Click **Print Area**.

4 Select **Set Print Area**.

◆ If you have a print area set, and wish to print a different range you can do so using print selection (see below).

If you have a print area set and wish to print the whole worksheet:

1 Click the Microsoft Office button.

2 Select **Print**, then **Print...** from the menu.

3 In the **Print** dialog box, select **Active sheet** in the **Print what** options.

4 Select the **Ignore print areas** checkbox.

5 Click **OK**.

To remove a print area:

1 Go to the **Page Setup** group on the **Page Layout** tab.

2 Click **Print Area**.

3 Select **Clear Print Area**.

• If you have a print area set, you can select additional cells and add them to the print area. These will normally be adjacent to those in the original print area.

Print Selection

You can print any part of your worksheet, whether a print area is set or not.

1 Select the range of cells you wish to print.

2 Click the Microsoft Office button and select **Print**, then **Print...** from the menu.

3 In the **Print** dialog box, select **Selection** in the **Print what** options.

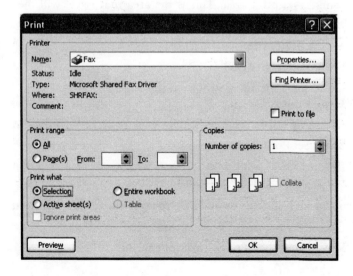

To preview before printing:

1 Click the **Preview** button.

2 Check the layout and breaks, and if you are happy with them, click **OK** to print.

Breaks

Page breaks are inserted automatically by Excel if your data will not fit onto one sheet of paper. If the automatic page breaks do not occur exactly where you would want them, you can insert manual page breaks.

To insert a horizontal page break:

◆ Select the row (or select the cell in column A) below which you want to insert a page break.

To insert a vertical page break:

◆ Select the column (or select the cell in row 1) to the right of which you want to insert a page break.

To insert a horizontal and vertical page break at the same time:

1 Select the cell immediately below and to the right of where you want to start a new page.

2 Click the **Breaks** button on the **Page Setup** group.

3 Select **Insert Page Break**.

◆ A page break will be inserted above the current row or to the left of the current column.

Breaks

| Insert Page Break |
| Remove Page Break |
| Reset All Page Breaks |

To remove a page break:

1 Select any cell in the row below the page break you wish to remove.

Or

◆ Select any cell in the column to the right of the page break you wish to remove.

2 Click the **Breaks** button on the **Page Setup** group.

3 Select **Remove Page Break**.

To remove all page breaks:

1 Select any cell in your worksheet.

2 Click the **Breaks** button on the **Page Setup** group.

3 Select **Reset All Page Breaks**.

Background

The Background option lets you display an image on the background of your worksheet. This can improve the appearance of the screen or of a web page, but note that these do not print.

1 Select any cell in the worksheet.

2 Click the **Background** button on the **Page Setup** group.

3 Browse through your folders until you find the image you wish to use.

4 Select the image.

5 Click **Insert**.

* To remove a background, click the **Delete Background** button (the Background button changes to this when a background is applied).

* Depending on the background selected, you may find it difficult to read your data with this formatting applied. You could try hiding the gridlines, or applying a fill colour to cells with data to improve readability.

Print Titles

If you are printing a worksheet with a list of data that runs over several pages, you might find the printout easier to read if you have the column and/or row titles repeated on each page.

1 Click **Print Titles** in the **Page Setup** group.

2 On the **Sheet** tab, specify the rows and/or columns that you want to repeat on each page.

* Click and drag on the row numbers or column letters (move the dialog box if necessary, so you can see them) or type them, e.g. $1:$4 for rows 1–4, or $A:$B for columns A and B.

3 Click **OK**.

Page Setup dialog box

Many of the options discussed in this section can be found on the various tabs in the Page Setup dialog box.

You can access this dialog box from several places by clicking the dialog box launcher button that is in most of the groups on the Page Layout tab.

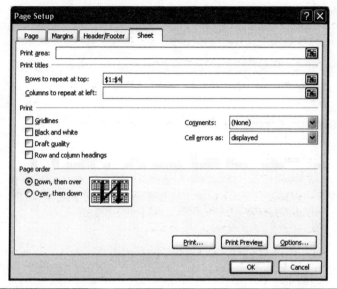

Scale to Fit

If a worksheet is more than a page in size, you can specify the number of pages you want it to be printed on using the **Scale to Fit** group on the **Page Layout** tab.

* Specify the number of pages wide in the **Width** field and/or the number of pages high in the **Height** field.

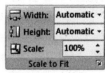

Or

* Leave both the Width and Height field at automatic, and set the percentage scaling that you wish to use.

Scaling can be very useful if the last page of your worksheet contains only a small amount of data. You can specify that the worksheet prints on one page less than it really needs – Excel will scale it down to fit onto that number of pages.

Page order

If your worksheet is going to print out on more than one sheet of paper, the pages can be printed down then over or over then down. You can specify the order you prefer.

1 Open the **Page Setup** dialog box – if you do so from the **Sheet Options** group, it will take you straight to the **Sheet** tab in the dialog box.

2 On the **Sheet** tab, select the **Page Order** option required.

3 Click **OK**.

Gridlines, row and column headings

When you print your worksheet out, the gridlines, row and column headings do not normally print. This is usually how you would want it, but there may be times when it is useful to print out the gridlines and/or the headings – for example, when printing out the formulas and functions (see Chapter 5).

To print the gridlines:

• Tick the **Print** checkbox in the **Gridlines** section of the **Sheet Options** group.

To print the row and column headings:

• Tick the **Print** option in the **Headings** section of the **Sheet Options** group.

Headers and footers

Headers and footers display information at the top or bottom of every page that prints out for your worksheet. They are useful for page numbers, your name, the date that the worksheet is printed, the worksheet name, the workbook name – or any other information that you would like to appear in them.

To add a header and/or footer to your pages:

1 Go to the **Insert** tab.

2 Click the **Header & Footer** button 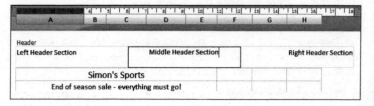 in the **Text** group.

3 The insertion point moves to the centre of the header, and the Header & Footer tools are displayed on the **Design** tab.

4 There are three sections to the header and footer area – left, middle and right. To move from one to another, click in it, or press [**Tab**] to cycle through the sections.

5 Type your header and/or footer in through the keyboard.

Or

6 To insert a standard header or footer, with combinations of the sheet name, workbook name and other elements, select one from the **Header** and **Footer** lists.

Or

7 To insert individual standard elements, click the appropriate button in the **Header & Footer** elements group.

To move between the Header and Footer area:

• Use the buttons in the Navigation group.

Other options are available in the **Options** group.

When you choose the Header & Footer command, Excel takes your worksheet into Page Layout view.

Summary

In this chapter we have discussed:

* Formatting using the Font group
* Formatting using the Alignment group
* Number formats
* The Format Painter
* Standard styles
* Conditional formatting
* Freezing panes
* Splitting the screen
* Margins, orientation, headers and footers and other page layout options.

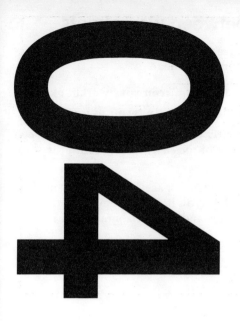

04

working with sheets

In this chapter you will learn:

- about worksheet layout
- how to insert, delete and rename worksheets
- about moving and copying worksheets
- how to group worksheets
- to change the tab colour

4.1 Moving between worksheets

The worksheet tabs appear at the bottom left of your screen – to the left of the horizontal scrollbar.

To move from one sheet to another in your workbook:

♦ Click the sheet tab of the sheet you want to work on.

If you can't see all the sheet tabs in the sheet tab bar, you can use the buttons to the left of the sheet tabs to scroll the sheet tabs into view.

You can change the amount of space allocated to the sheet tab bar and the horizontal scroll bar by dragging the tab split box between the sheet tabs and the horizontal scroll bar.

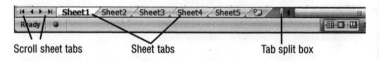

Scroll sheet tabs   Sheet tabs   Tab split box

4.2 Worksheet design

Before you start setting up a worksheet, you should give some thought to its design. The main areas to keep in mind are:

● Work out the purpose of your worksheet. Ask yourself:

  ♦ What do you want to communicate?

  ♦ What should be emphasized or de-emphasized?

  ♦ How will you show the relationship between areas?

● Keep it simple.

● Be consistent – within a worksheet and across worksheets. If you produce the same worksheet every month, regular readers will be able to find the information they need quickly if it's always in the same place.

● Use formatting and layout options to add contrast to different areas of your worksheet.

There are no hard and fast rules – the main objective is to display the data in a clear and unambiguous way. If you like your worksheet layout and your audience can understand it, it's probably OK.

Some Dos and Don'ts of worksheet design

DO make sure you use a font that is easy to read – Calibri (the default) is a very 'clean' font, Times New Roman is easy on the eye.

DO use 'white space' – leave some blank rows or columns between sections of your worksheet to make it easier to read.

DO use borders and/or shading effects to divide large worksheets up into manageable chunks and to draw attention to subtotals and totals.

DO format your numbers appropriately – currency, number of decimal places, percentage, etc.

DO make sure your worksheet is legible – don't use too small a font or shrink to fit data to the extent it is too small to read.

DO add comments to cells that need an explanation (see section 5.9).

DON'T use too many different fonts or sizes on a worksheet.

DON'T overdo font and fill colours – you'll give readers a headache!

DON'T print gridlines on a final report – they will give it a very cluttered look, though they may be useful on a draft print-out, or one with formulas displayed.

4.3   Themes

You can use themes to quickly and easily apply a set of predefined formats to worksheets and charts. The colours, fonts and effects contained in a theme have been carefully coordinated to give a professional look to your worksheets. A theme is a set of formatting options that includes a colour theme (a set of colours), a font theme (for headings and body text) and an effects theme (for lines and fill effects).

To change the theme:

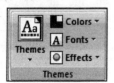

1   Click **Themes** in the **Themes** group on the **Page Layout** tab.

2   Select the theme that you want.

Initially, you will only see built-in themes to choose from. You may eventually create your own themes – if you do this you will also have the choice of custom themes.

When you change a theme, you will notice that the formatting options on your worksheet change to reflect the settings in the theme you select.

If you applied standard styles in Chapter 3, you will notice that the formatting options are stored in the style changes when you choose a different theme.

You can customize the individual elements of a theme – the colour, font or effect:

- Select the colour from the colour options.
- Select the font from the font options.
- Select the effect from the effect options.

4.4 Inserting worksheets

When you create a workbook in Excel the default number of worksheets is three. This may be (more than) enough, but if you need more than three you can easily add them.

To insert a worksheet:

- Click the **New Worksheet** button to the right of the sheet tabs. A sheet will be added to the end of the workbook.

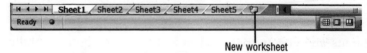

New worksheet

Default sheets in a workbook

If you regularly need to add (or remove) worksheets to get the right number of worksheets in your workbook, you could change the default number of worksheets to a number that is more appropriate for you.

To change the default number of sheets:

1 Click the Microsoft Office button and choose **Excel Options** from the menu.

2 Go to the **Popular** options.

3 Specify the default number of sheets required.

4 Click **OK**.

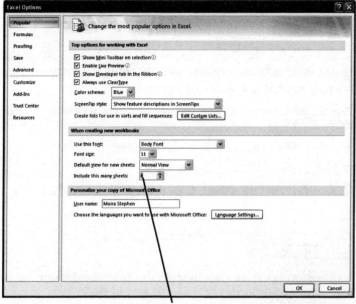

Default number of sheets

4.5 Deleting worksheets

If a workbook has too many sheets you can delete any you don't need.

To delete a worksheet:

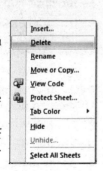

1 Right-click on the sheet tab of the sheet you want to delete.

2 Select **Delete** from the shortcut menu.

♦ If the sheet contains data, you will be asked to confirm the deletion.

3 Respond to the prompt – click **Delete** if you really want to delete the sheet, **Cancel** if you change your mind.

Be careful when deleting sheets – **Undo** will not restore them!

4.6 Renaming worksheets

By default, worksheets are named *Sheet1*, *Sheet2*, etc. If you only use one or two sheets in a workbook this may cause you no problems. If you have several worksheets, life will be easier if you give them a name that actually means something.

To rename a worksheet:

1 Double-click on the sheet tab you want to rename.

2 Type in the name you want to use.

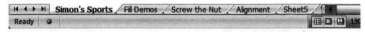

3 Press [**Enter**] or click anywhere on the worksheet.

4.7 Moving and copying worksheets

To move or copy a worksheet within a workbook, you can use drag and drop techniques.

To move a worksheet:

• Click and drag the worksheet tab of the sheet you want to move along the sheet tabs until it is in the correct place.

To copy a worksheet:

• Click on a worksheet tab, hold down [**Ctrl**] and drag it to the required position. The name will have (2) after it, to show that the new sheet is a copy. Rename it as required.

To move or copy a worksheet to another workbook:

• If you are moving or copying a worksheet to a different workbook, open this one before you start.

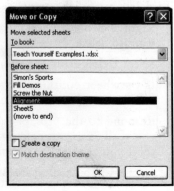

1 Right-click on the tab of the sheet to move or copy.

2 Choose **Move** or **Copy** from the shortcut menu.

3 At the dialog box, select the workbook you wish to move or copy to.

4 Specify where in the workbook you want the worksheet moved or copied to.

5 Tick the checkbox if you want to copy rather than move.

6 Click **OK**.

4.8 Grouping worksheets

There may be times when you want to enter the same text, data or formulas into corresponding cells in more than one worksheet. You could enter your work onto one worksheet, then copy it onto the others, or you could group the worksheets and enter the standard text, data, formula and/or functions that will appear on them all. You then ungroup the sheets to add the elements that are unique to each one.

When worksheets are grouped, anything you do on one sheet is automatically replicated in every sheet in the group.

To group adjacent worksheets:

1 Click on the tab of the first sheet you want in the group.

2 Hold down [**Shift**] and click on the last tab in the group.

To group non-adjacent worksheets:

1 Click on the tab of the first sheet in the group.

2 Hold down [Ctrl] and click on each sheet tab that you want in the group.

To select all worksheets:

1 Right-click on any sheet tab.

2 Click **Select all sheets**.

When worksheets are grouped the word [Group] appears on the workbook title bar.

To ungroup worksheets:

1 Click on any worksheet tab that isn't part of the group.

Or

2 Right-click on one of the grouped worksheet tabs.

3 Choose **Ungroup Sheets** from the pop-up menu.

4.9 Tab colour

If you have several worksheets in a book (or related worksheets across books) you may find colouring the sheet tabs to be useful.

To change the tab colour:

1 Select the tab(s) that you want to colour.

2 Right-click on the selected tabs and choose **Tab Color...**

3 Select a colour.

4 Click **OK**.

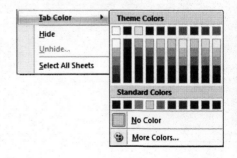

Summary

In this chapter we have discussed:

+ Moving between sheets in a workbook

+ Worksheet layout and design

+ Themes

+ Inserting worksheets

+ Default number of sheets

+ Deleting and renaming sheets

+ Moving and copying sheets

+ Grouping sheets

+ Changing the tab colour.

05

formulas and functions

In this chapter you will learn:

- more about functions and formulas
- about relative and absolute addresses and circular references
- how to use named ranges
- how to add comments and protect your worksheet

5.1 AutoSum

The worksheet below contains details of quarterly sales figures. Enter the text and data into a new worksheet in your workbook. We need to calculate the total sales figures for each sales representative for the year and also the total sales figure for each quarter.

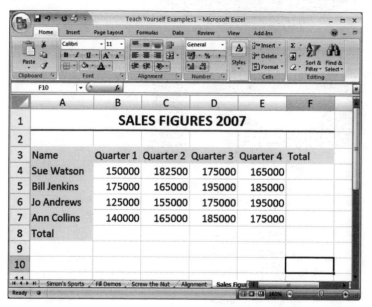

You could use a formula to calculate the total (e.g. in **F4** you might have **=B4+C4+D4+E4**), but the easist and quickest way to calculate it is with AutoSum.

To calculate the totals using AutoSum:

1 Select a cell to the right of a row or below a column of figures that you want to add, e.g. in cell F4 or cell B8.

2 Click the **AutoSum** button in the **Editing** group on the **Home** tab.

Or

◆ Click the **AutoSum** button on the **Formulas** tab.

3 The range of cells to be added together will be highlighted. Note that the function also appears in the Formula bar.

4 If the suggested range of cells is correct, press [**Enter**].

Or

* If the suggested range is *not* the range of cells you want to add, drag over the correct range, then press [**Enter**].

The total value of the selected range will appear in the active cell when you accept the formula by pressing [**Enter**].

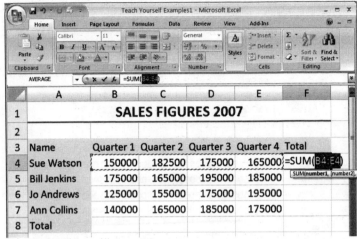

* Excel calculates the total value of the selected cells using the SUM function. Its syntax is **=SUM (cell range)** – you could type in the function, but it's usually easier (and less error prone) to use AutoSum.

You could select each of the total cells in turn and use AutoSum to calculate the values that should appear in them, or use AutoFill (see section 2.11) to copy the function down or across the other total cells.

	A	B	C	D	E	F
1			**SALES FIGURES 2007**			
2						
3	Name	Quarter 1	Quarter 2	Quarter 3	Quarter 4	Total
4	Sue Watson	£150,000	£182,500	£175,000	£165,000	£ 672,500
5	Bill Jenkins	£175,000	£165,000	£195,000	£185,000	£ 720,000
6	Jo Andrews	£125,000	£155,000	£175,000	£195,000	£ 650,000
7	Ann Collins	£140,000	£165,000	£185,000	£175,000	£ 665,000
8	Total	£590,000	£667,500	£730,000	£720,000	£2,707,500

To AutoSum several groups of cells simultaneously:

1 Select all of the rows and columns to total, and the cells to contain the results of the AutoSum calculations.

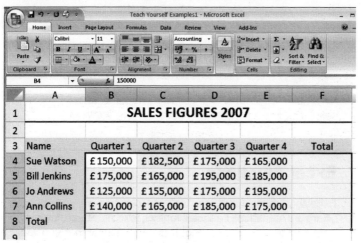

2 Click the **AutoSum** button **Σ ▾**.

The cells in the rightmost column and bottom row of the selected area will each have the Sum function inserted into them.

Non-adjacent cells

You can also use AutoSum to total non-adjacent cells if you wish.

To total non-adjacent cells:

1 Select the cell that will contain the result of the calculation.

2 Click the **AutoSum** button **Σ ▾**.

3 Click on the first cell you want to include in the range.

4 Hold down [**Ctrl**] and click on each of the other cells to be included in the function.

5 Press [**Enter**].

◆ To type in the function, start with = (equals sign). A range of adjacent cells has the first cell address in the range, followed by : (colon), then the last address in the range. The addresses for non-adjacent cells must be separated by , (comma).

Excel functions

Excel has many functions that you can use on your data. There are statistical, financial, logical, text, database, lookup, data and time functions, etc. It is very unlikely that you will need to use them all (you'll be glad to know), but we'll look at some that are useful at a general level. You can then go on and explore the functions and find any that may be useful in your particular situation. Use the online Help as necessary.

5.2 Common statistical functions

The most commonly used statistical functions – average, count, maximum and minimum – can be found in the AutoSum list. To display this, click the arrow on either of the AutoSum buttons.

Min	returns the smallest value
Max	returns the highest value
Average	returns the mean value (=total/count)
Count Numbers	returns the number of numeric entries

There are lots of other statistical functions to be found in the Insert Function dialog box (see section 5.3). You can display the dialog box by clicking **More Functions...** at the bottom of the AutoSum list.

A useful statistical function not on the AutoSum list is **CountA**, which returns the number of numeric or text entries – it counts all cells that are not empty.

The Average, Count Numbers, CountA, Min and Max work in exactly the same way as the Sum function in the AutoSum list.

1 Select the cell that the result will be displayed in.

2 Choose the function required from the AutoSum list.

3 Drag over the cells (or [Ctrl]-click) that the function will use.

4 Press [Enter].

◆ Try them out on your Simon's Sports data.

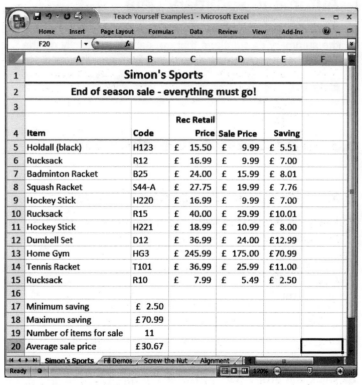

Display these values:

◆ **Minimum** from the saving column.

◆ **Maximum** from the saving column.

- **Number** of items on sale.
- **Average** sale price of the items in the list.

To edit a function:

1 Select the cell that contains the function.

2 Edit the function in the Formula bar.

Or

- Click the **Insert Function** button again to display the **Function Arguments** dialog box.

Automatic summary data

When you select a range of cells that contains data, notice the summary calculations that appear automatically on the Status bar. The Average, Count and Sum are displayed.

5.3 Insert Function dialog box

To insert a function:

1 Select the cell that you want the function to go in.

2 Click the **Insert Function** button 🔧 (to the left of the Formula bar).

Or

1 Click the drop-down arrow to the right of the AutoSum tool.

2 Select **More Functions...** from the list.

Or

1 Press [=].

2 Click the drop-down arrow at the top of the functions list.

3 Choose **More Functions...**

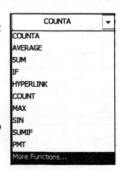

- The **Insert Function** dialog box is displayed.

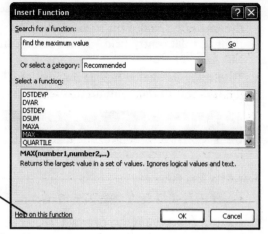

Click for help on the selected function

To search for a function:

1 Type what you want to do in the **Search for a function** field.

2 Click **Go**.

♦ Excel will display a list of 'Recommended' functions.

3 Select a function from the list and click **OK**.

To select a function (without searching):

1 Select the category (choose **All** if you're not sure which one).

2 Scroll through the list to find the function.

3 Select it and click **OK**.

♦ The **Function Arguments** dialog box appears.

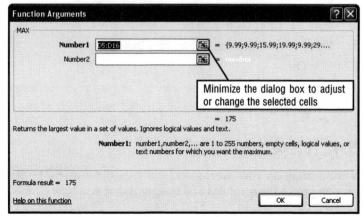

- If the **Function Arguments** dialog box obscures the area of the worksheet you want to view, click the 🔳 button to the right of a data entry field – it will become minimized, so you can see your worksheet.

- To display the dialog box again, click the **Restore** button at the far right of the minimized window.

Restore

To edit a function:

1 Select the cell that contains the function.

2 Edit the function in the Formula bar.

Or

- Click the **Insert Function** button again to display the **Function Arguments** dialog box.

Recently used functions list

You can quickly add recently-used functions to the Formula bar using the Function list.

1 Select the cell where you want the function to go.

2 Type '='.

3 The **Name** box changes to a Function list.

4 Click the drop-down arrow to the right of the list.

5 Select the function required.

6 Complete the **Function Arguments** dialog box.

7 Click **OK**.

- **More Functions...** at the bottom of the list opens the **Insert Function** dialog box.

5.4 View formulas

When setting up your worksheet, it is sometimes useful to display and print the formulas and functions that you have entered into the cells.

Each formula or function is displayed in the formula bar when its cell is selected, but you can get Excel to display all the formulas and functions in your worksheet if you wish.

To switch the display of formulas and functions on and off:

1 Display the **Formulas** tab on the Ribbon.

2 Click the **View Formulas** button 🔣 in the **Formula Auditing** group.

Or

◆ Use the keyboard shortcut [**Ctrl**]-[**'**] (at the top left of the keyboard, above [**Tab**]).

The formulas and functions used in the Simon's Sports worksheet are displayed below – note that what you can see is the data exactly as it is entered, and not as it is displayed on the screen.

	Teach Yourself Examples1 - Microsoft Excel			
Home	Insert	Page Layout	Formulas	Data	Review	View	Add-Ins

F20

	A	B	C	D	E
1	Simon's Sports				
2	End of season sale - everything must go!				
3					
4	Item	Code	Rec Retail Price	Sale Price	Saving
5	Holdall (black)	H123	15.5	9.99	=C5-D5
6	Rucksack	R12	16.99	9.99	=C6-D6
7	Badminton Racket	B25	24	15.99	=C7-D7
8	Squash Racket	S44-A	27.75	19.99	=C8-D8
9	Hockey Stick	H220	16.99	9.99	=C9-D9
10	Rucksack	R15	40	29.99	=C10-D10
11	Hockey Stick	H221	18.99	10.99	=C11-D11
12	Dumbell Set	D12	36.99	24	=C12-D12
13	Home Gym	HG3	245.99	175	=C13-D13
14	Tennis Racket	T101	36.99	25.99	=C14-D14
15	Rucksack	R10	7.99	5.49	=C15-D15
16					
17	Minimum saving	=MIN(E5:E15)			
18	Maximum saving	=MAX(E5:E15)			
19	Number of items for sale	=COUNT(C5:C15)			
20	Average sale price	=AVERAGE(D5:D15)			

5.5 Formula Auditing

You can use the command buttons in the Formula Auditing groups to identify:

♦ which cells are *dependent* on others, i.e. are calculated using values in other cells.

♦ which cell values are *precedents*, i.e. are used to calculate the values held in other cells.

You can quickly trace the precedents and dependents of a cell using the Formula Auditing commands.

1 Select a cell that contains a formula or function.

2 Click the **Trace Precedents** button [🔲⇨ Trace Precedents] to identify which cells affect the value of the selected cell.

3 Click the **Trace Dependents** button [⇦🔲 Trace Dependents] to identify which cells are affected by the value in the selected cell.

	Teach Yourself Examples1 - Microsoft Excel					
Home	Insert	Page Layout	Formulas	Data	Review	View	Add-Ins

E14   =C14-D14

	A	B	C	D	E	F
1	**Simon's Sports**					
2	**End of season sale - everything must go!**					
3						
4	**Item**	**Code**	**Rec Retail Price**	**Sale Price**	**Saving**	
5	Holdall (black)	H123	£ 15.50	£ 9.99	£ 5.51	
6	Rucksack	R12	£ 16.99	£ 9.99	£ 7.00	
7	Badminton Racket	B25	£ 24.00	£ 15.99	£ 8.01	
8	Squash Racket	S44-A	£ 27.75	£ 19.99	£ 7.76	
9	Hockey Stick	H220	£ 16.99	£ 9.99	£ 7.00	
10	Rucksack	R15	£ 40.00	£ 29.99	£10.01	
11	Hockey Stick	H221	£ 18.99	£ 10.99	£ 8.00	
12	Dumbell Set	D12	£ 36.99	£ 24.00	£12.99	
13	Home Gym	HG3	£ 245.99	£ 175.00	£70.99	
14	Tennis Racket	T101	£ 36.99	£ 25.99	£11.00	
15	Rucksack	R10	£ 7.99	£ 5.49	£ 2.50	
16						
17	Minimum saving	£ 2.50				
18	Maximum saving	£70.99				
19	Number of items for sale	11				
20	Average sale price	£30.67				

To remove the arrows:

* Click the drop-down arrow to the right of the **Remove Arrows** button and select from the options.

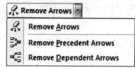

5.6 Relative and absolute addresses

You will have noticed that when you AutoFill or copy a formula, the addresses in it change automatically, relative to the position you copy them to. By default, the cell addresses used are *relative addresses*. There will be times when you use a cell address in a formula, and want to copy the formula down some rows or across some columns, but don't want the address to change relative to its new position.

In the next example, we are going to calculate the income from admissions to a film centre.

* Enter the data onto a new worksheet (see section 4.4 to add a new sheet). DO NOT complete the *Revenue* columns – we will enter formulas to calculate those figures.

Teach Yourself Examples1 - Microsoft Excel

Home · Insert · Page Layout · Formulas · Data · Review · View · Add-Ins

H15

	A	B	C	D	E	F	G
1			**SOUTHSIDE FILM CENTRE**				
2			**MONTHLY INCOME FROM ADMISSIONS**				
3							
4			**Admission Charges**				
5			Adult	£5.50			
6			OAP	£4.00			
7			Concessions	£3.50			
8							
9			January		February		March
10		Number	Revenue	Number	Revenue	Number	Revenue
11	Adult	2500		1950		2400	
12	OAP	3400		2750		3200	
13	Concession	3950		3500		4300	
14							

To calculate the January revenue figures:

1 Enter a formula into the *Adult* cell in the *January, Revenue* column to calculate the income from this group. The first revenue figure for January is calculated by multiplying the number of adults (B11) by the adult admission rate (D5). The formula in C11 should be =B11*D5.

2 Use AutoFill (see section 2.11) to copy the formula down over the *OAP* and *Concession* cells.

We could enter the appropriate formulas into the February and March columns in a similar way. However, it would be quicker to *copy* the January formulas. This poses two problems:

♦ We **don't** want the D5 (adult rate), D6 (OAP rate), D7 (concession rate) addresses to change when we copy the formula.

♦ We can't use AutoFill because the cells we want to copy to are not next to the source cells.

To stop a cell address from changing when we copy it, we must create an *absolute address*. This will not change when the formula or function containing it is copied or moved.

To create an absolute cell address:

♦ Enter a $ sign in front of each coordinate you want to fix. Type the '$' sign, or use [F4].

To absolutely address the cells in a formula:

1 Select the cell that contains the formula (C11, C12 or C13 in this example) – the formula appears in the Formula bar.

2 Click in the Formula bar.

3 Place the insertion point to the *right* of the cell address you want to make absolute (D5 or D6 or D7).

4 Press [F4] until you have the cell addressed properly.

	f_x	=$D$5*B11

♦ Each time you press [F4] it moves through the absolute addressing options.

$D$5	neither coordinate will change
D$5	the column will change if you copy the formula across columns
$D5	the row number will change if you copy the formula down rows
D5	both coordinates will change relative to its new position

Absolutely address the admission rate cell address in each of the January formulas.

Once you've made the appropriate addresses absolute, you can copy the formula across to the February and March columns.

To complete the February and March figures:

1 Select the cells you are copying from – the *January* revenue figures in this case, C11:C13.

2 Click the **Copy** button in the **Clipboard** group of the **Home** tab (or use [**Ctrl**]-[**C**]).

3 Select the first cell you want to paste into, e.g. E11 for the *February* figures – you don't need to select E11:E13.

4 Click the **Paste** button in the **Clipboard** group (or use [**Ctrl**]-[**V**]).

5 Select cell G11 as the first cell for the *March* figures.

6 Paste the data again.

7 Press [**Esc**] on your keyboard to cancel the copy routine.

Your final worksheet should look similar to the ones below and overleaf. The first picture displays the formulas (you may have different cell addresses if you have used different rows and columns for your data), the second one shows the results.

			Teach Yourself Examples1 - Microsoft Excel			
	Home	Insert	Page Layout	Formulas	Data Review View	Add-Ins
	H15					
	A	B	C	D	E	F	G
1			**SOUTHSIDE FILM CENTRE**				
2			**MONTHLY INCOME FROM ADMISSIONS**				
3							
4			**Admission Charges**				
5			Adult	5.5			
6			OAP	4			
7			Concessions	3.5			
8							
9			January		February		March
10		Number	Revenue	Number	Revenue	Number	Revenue
11	Adult	2500	=$D$5*B11	1950	=$D$5*D11	2400	=$D$5*F11
12	OAP	3400	=$D$6*B12	2750	=$D$6*D12	3200	=$D$6*F12
13	Concession	3950	=$D$7*B13	3500	=$D$7*D13	4300	=$D$7*F13

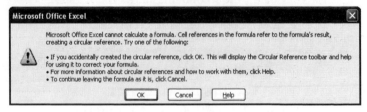

				SOUTHSIDE FILM CENTRE		
	A	B	C	D	E	F	G

	A	B	C	D	E	F	G
1			**SOUTHSIDE FILM CENTRE**				
2			**MONTHLY INCOME FROM ADMISSIONS**				
3							
4			Admission Charges				
5			Adult	£5.50			
6			OAP	£4.00			
7			Concessions	£3.50			
8							
9			January		February		March
10		Number	Revenue	Number	Revenue	Number	Revenue
11	Adult	2500	£13,750.00	1950	£10,725.00	2400	£13,200.00
12	OAP	3400	£13,600.00	2750	£11,000.00	3200	£12,800.00
13	Concession	3950	£13,825.00	3500	£12,250.00	4300	£15,050.00

5.7 Circular references

If you create a formula that refers to its own cell, you have a *circular reference*. Excel cannot resolve these using normal calculation methods and a warning will appear should one occur.

Click OK and read the Help page that appears, and minimize it so that you can refer back to it quickly if necessary.

To review and amend the circular references:

1 If you look at the status bar, it will tell you where the circular reference is – if there is no cell address displayed, it means that the cell causing the problem is not on the current worksheet.

2 Go to the problem cell – click on it or go to the **Formula** tab, and in the **Formula Editing** group, click the arrow beside

Error Checking, select Circular References, then the first cell reference displayed.

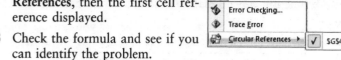

3 Check the formula and see if you can identify the problem.

* If the current cell address is in the formula, you have found the problem – amend it – no cell should contain a formula that refers to itself.

4 If you can't see the error, go to the next cell that is identified as being a problem cell.

5 Continue until you have located and fixed the error.

* When the circular reference problem is resolved, the circular reference prompt will disappear from the status bar.

Some engineering and scientific formulas require circular references – in this case you may need to change the number of iterations (the number of times Excel recalculates the sheet).

To change the number of iterations:

1 Click the Microsoft Office button.

2 Select Excel Options, and then choose Excel Options.

3 In the Formulas section, under Calculation Options, select the Enable iterative calculation checkbox.

4 Type the number of iterations in the Maximum iterations box – the higher the number the more time Excel needs to calculate the worksheet.

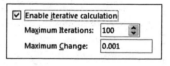

5 You can set the maximum amount of change you will accept in the Maximum Change box. The smaller the number, the more accurate the result, and the longer Excel needs to perform the calculation.

5.8 Named ranges

When building up your formulas and functions, you have been using cell addresses to tell Excel which cells you want to use in your calculations. Cell addresses are not really very user-friendly

– it isn't always immediately clear what the formula **=B13*$B$6** or the function **=AVERAGE(D5:D17)** is actually doing.

To make your worksheet easier to understand you can use *named ranges* instead of cell addresses in your formulas and functions.

There are two main ways of naming ranges.

You can either:

♦ Use the existing labels that are on your worksheet to refer to the related data.

Or

♦ Create new descriptive names.

Create named ranges

You can easily give a cell or range of cells a name. The name used can be anything you like (as long as it obeys the rules below) or you can use column and/or row labels as names for your cell ranges. Named ranges that you create are available to any worksheet within the workbook.

Rules for naming ranges:

♦ The maximum size for a name is 255 characters.

♦ Spaces are not allowed (use an underline or a full stop to separate words).

♦ The first character in a name *must* be a letter or an underline character (other characters can be letters, numbers, full stops and underlines, but not commas, question marks or other punctuation characters).

♦ You *cannot* use a cell reference for a range name, e.g. B75 or AA$24.

♦ Names can contain upper and lower case letters. Excel is *not* case sensitive. If you create a name called *Profit*, then another called *PROFIT*, the second will replace the first.

To name cells using the existing row and column headings:

1 Select the row (or column) headings and the cells to be named.

2 Click **Create from Selection** in the **Named Cells** group.

3 Select the location of the names you wish to use in the **Create Names from Selection** dialog box.

4 Click **OK**.

♦ The scope of the named ranges is the workbook when you use this method.

To name a cell or range without using headings:

1 Select the cell or range of cells you want to name.

2 Click the **Name** box at the left edge of the Formula bar.

3 Type in a name for the cells.

4 Press [**Enter**].

♦ When you name cells in this way the scope of the named range is the workbook.

Or

1 Select the cells you want to name.

2 In the **Named Cells** group on the **Formula** tab, click the **Name a Range** button (or drop down the **Name a Range** options and choose *Name a Range...*).

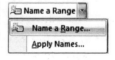

3 Enter the name to give the cell(s) in the **Name** field.

4 Specify the **Scope** of the named range – it could be the whole workbook, or a specific worksheet.

5 The range will be completed using the range of cells selected – edit if necessary.

6 Click **OK**.

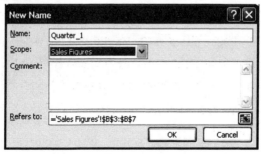

- If you limit the scope of a named range to a particular worksheet it will only be available in that worksheet.

You could try naming ranges for:

- the columns in the *Screw the Nut plc* worksheet.

- the admission charges in the *Film Centre* worksheet, with names such as *Adult_rate*, *OAP_rate*, and *Con_rate*.

You can easily paste range names into your formula or function, rather than using the cell addresses.

To use a range name in a formula or function:

1 Select the cell that will contain your formula or function.

2 Start entering the formula or function in the normal way.

3 When you want to specify the range that you wish to use, click the **Use in formula** button in the **Named Cells** group and select the named range from the list.

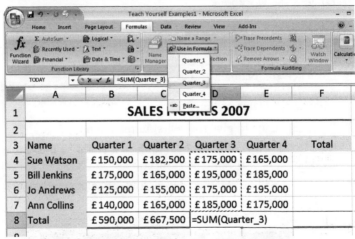

- Edit some formulas to use range names instead of addresses.

If you no longer use a range name, you can delete it. Deleting the range name does not delete the cell contents, but it will affect any cells that refer to the named range in a formula.

To delete a range name:

1 Click **Name Manager** in the **Named Cells** group.

2 Select the named range you no longer require.

3 Click **Delete**.

4 You will be prompted to confirm the deletion – click **OK**.

5 Close the **Name Manager** dialog box.

If you delete a named range that is used in a formula, this error message is displayed in the cell.

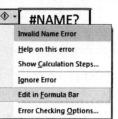

#NAME?

You can check out the options for dealing with the error using the SmartTag that appears to the left of the cell – and **Invalid Name Error** is obviously the problem.

Amend the formula or function to reference the appropriate cell address again.

Applying named ranges

If you have created your formulas using cell addresses, and then decide to use named ranges, you can easily convert the addresses to range names.

To use this feature, the scope of the named range must be the worksheet.

1 To convert all of the cell addresses in your formulas to named ranges, select any single cell in your worksheet.

Or

2 To convert only part of your worksheet, select the range.

3 Choose **Apply Names...** from the **Name a Range** drop-down list.

4 Select the names you want to apply.

5 Click **OK**.

- Experiment with named ranges – they are really handy as they can make your worksheets much easier to understand.
- The Sales Figures worksheet below was updated by creating named ranges, then using the Apply Names feature.

	A	B	C	D	E
1			SALES FIGURES 2007		
2					
3	Name	Quarter 1	Quarter 2	Quarter 3	Quarter 4
4	Sue Watson	150000	182500	175000	165000
5	Bill Jenkins	175000	165000	195000	185000
6	Jo Andrews	125000	155000	175000	195000
7	Ann Collins	140000	165000	185000	175000
8	Total	=SUM(Quarter_1)	=SUM(Quarter_2)	=SUM(Quarter_3)	=SUM(Quarter_4)

(Teach Yourself Examples1 - Microsoft Excel — Home, Insert, Page Layout, Formulas, Data, Review, View, Add-Ins — E11)

- You can also edit a named range from the **Name Manager** dialog box.

5.9 Comments

If you think that the purpose of a formula in a cell is not self explicit, you can add a note – called a 'comment' – to the cell. You will find them particularly useful if you don't use named ranges, and want to add an explanation to a cell, or, if others share your worksheets and you want to explain the logic behind an entry you have made.

To add a comment to a cell:

1 Select the cell you want to add a comment to.

2 On the **Review** tab on the Ribbon, click **New Comment** in the **Comments** group.

3 Type your comment into the comment box.

4 Click outside the box.

- A small red triangle will appear in the top right corner of your cell to indicate that it has a comment attached.

To edit an existing comment:

1 Select the cell that the comment is attached to.

2 Click the **Edit Comment** button in the **Comments** group.

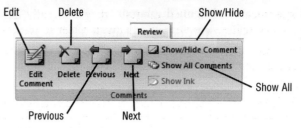

Edit   Delete   Show/Hide

Previous   Next

3 Edit the text and click outside the box.

To delete a comment:

1 Select the cell that the comment is attached to.

2 Click the **Delete** button in the **Comments** group.

♦ If your worksheet contains several comments, you can move through your worksheet, jumping from one comment to the next using the **Previous** and **Next** buttons.

If you want a comment to remain visible on your screen when you move off the cell that it is attached to:

1 Select the cell.

2 Click the **Show/Hide Comment** button to toggle the display.

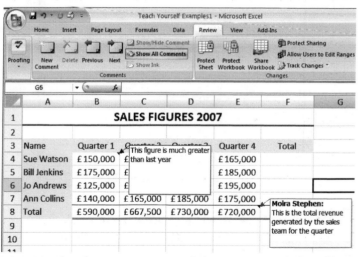

The name that appears automatically in a comment is taken from the user name in the Excel Options. You can edit or delete the name in the comment if you wish.

If you want all comments displayed:

- Click the **Show All Comments** button (click it again to hide them all).

To format a comment:

1 Show the comment.

2 Go to the **Home** tab, select the **Comment,** then click the drop-down arrow beside **Format** in the **Cells** group, and choose **Format Comment** from the options.

Or

3 Select the comment and press [Ctrl]-[1].

4 Format the lines and/or fill using the options on the **Colors and Lines** tab.

5 Click **OK**.

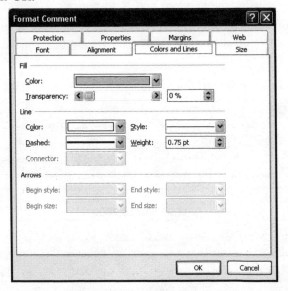

5.10 Worksheet protection

Having gone to the trouble of setting up formulas and functions on your worksheet, it would be a pity if they were accidentally overwritten when entering text and data. You can protect your worksheet to avoid this unfortunate situation arising.

When you protect a worksheet, cells formatted as locked cannot be edited, cells formatted as unlocked can. Initially all cells are locked. You must therefore unlock cells that you want to be able to edit in the protected sheet, before you protect the sheet.

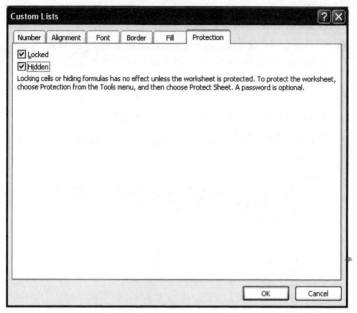

You may sometimes want to hide your formulas – especially if others are using the worksheets. If cells are formatted as hidden, the formula does not appear in the Formula bar when the cell is selected, or when the sheet is in Formula view once the worksheet protection has been activated.

To unlock cells:

1 Select the cells that you want unlocked.

2 On the **Home** tab, in the **Cells** group, click **Format,** then **Cells.**

3 Select the **Protection** tab in the **Format Cells** dialog box.

4 Clear the **Locked** checkbox.

To hide cell formulas:

1 Select the cells whose formulas you want to hide.

2 On the **Home** tab, in the **Cells** group, click **Format,** then **Cells.**

3 Select the **Protection** tab.

4 Tick the **Hidden** checkbox.

To activate the protection:

1 In the **Cells** group on the **Home** tab, click **Format**, then **Protect Sheet...**

2 If you wish to give your protection a password, enter it in the dialog box – just don't forget it!

3 Select the options you want made available to the user.

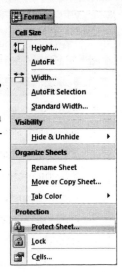

4 Click **OK**.

5 If you have given a password, re-enter it at the prompt and click **OK** again.

To deactivate the protection:

1 In the **Cells** group of the **Home** tab, click **Format**, then **Unprotect sheet...**

2 If you used a password, enter it at the prompt.

3 Click **OK**.

Summary

In this chapter we have introduced the most commonly used functions, and several features that are useful when working with formulas and functions. We have discussed:

* AutoSum

* Sum, Min, Max, Average, Count and CountA

* Using the Insert Function dialog box

* Viewing formulas on your worksheet

* Formula auditing

* Relative and absolute addresses

* Circular references

* Creating and using named ranges

* Using comments to explain the contents of cells

* Protecting your worksheet

* Locking and unlocking cells

* Hiding cell formulas.

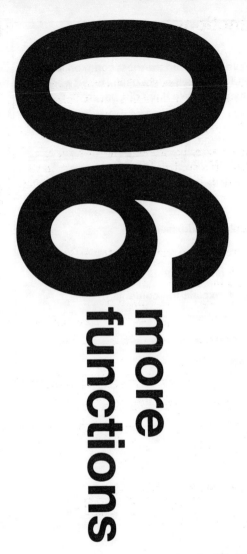

06

more functions

In this chapter you will learn:

- about Logical, Statistical, Math, Text, Date and Financial functions
- how to use Lookup tables
- about data tables, scenarios and PivotTables

6.1 Logical functions

IF function

The IF function is used to return one value if the condition you specify is True, and another value if the condition is False. The values returned can be text, numbers, or the result of a formula or function.

For example, you might be entering student end-of-term exam results into your worksheet. If a student has 50% or more in the exam, a pass will be awarded, if less than 50% is achieved, the result is a fail.

Comparison operators

Comparison operators are used in many functions. The next example uses one to check if the *Total Mark* is greater than or equal to 50. The operators include:

=	equal to	<>	not equal to
>	greater than	>=	greater than or equal to
<	less than	<=	less than or equal to

Enter this data into a new worksheet.

To return a 'Pass' or 'Fail' message in the *Result* column, we need to enter the IF function. You can use either cell addresses or named ranges in the function. In this example, the C4:C13 range has been named *Mark_awarded*.

To enter the function:

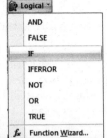

1 Select the first cell in the result column.

2 On the **Formulas** tab, click **Logical** in the **Function Library**.

3 Select **IF**.

4 In the **Function Arguments** dialog box, enter the condition to be evaluated in the **Logical test** field (Mark_awarded>=50).

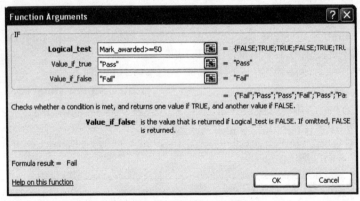

5 Specify the value if the condition is found to be True – you don't need to type in the quotes – Excel will enter them automatically as it builds the formula.

6 Specify the value if the condition is found to be False.

7 Click **OK**.

Arguments

The values used by functions to perform calculations or operations are called arguments. An argument may be a numeric value, a text value, a cell reference, a range of cells, a named range, or a nested function (a function within a function, see Nested IFs on page 108).

- AutoFill the function down through the Result column – Pass
  will appear in the rows where the condition is true, Fail will
  appear in the rows where the condition is false.

	D4		fx	=IF(Mark_awarded>=50,"Pass","Fail")	
	A	B	C	D	E
1	END OF TERM EXAM RESULTS				
2					
3	Firstname	Surname	Mark awarded	Result	
4	Gill	McLaren	45	Fail	
5	Pauline	Watson	65	Pass	
6	William	Smith	72	Pass	
7	Ann	Allan	48	Fail	
8	Andrew	Borthwick	52	Pass	
9	Peter	Jackson	91	Pass	
10	Alison	Smith	50	Pass	
11	Marion	Williamson	49	Fail	
12	Hector	Smith	68	Pass	
13	David	Watson	59	Pass	
14					

With the formulas displayed, the worksheet should look like the
illustration below. This example uses named ranges rather than
cell addresses. If we had used cell addresses the function would
have been =IF(C4>=50, "PASS", "FAIL"), etc.

	E13		fx	
	A	B	C	D
1	END OF TERM EXAM RESULTS			
2				
3	Firstname	Surname	Mark awarded	Result
4	Gill	McLaren	45	=IF(Mark_awarded>=50,"Pass","Fail")
5	Pauline	Watson	65	=IF(Mark_awarded>=50,"Pass","Fail")
6	William	Smith	72	=IF(Mark_awarded>=50,"Pass","Fail")
7	Ann	Allan	48	=IF(Mark_awarded>=50,"Pass","Fail")
8	Andrew	Borthwick	52	=IF(Mark_awarded>=50,"Pass","Fail")
9	Peter	Jackson	91	=IF(Mark_awarded>=50,"Pass","Fail")
10	Alison	Smith	50	=IF(Mark_awarded>=50,"Pass","Fail")
11	Marion	Williamson	49	=IF(Mark_awarded>=50,"Pass","Fail")
12	Hector	Smith	68	=IF(Mark_awarded>=50,"Pass","Fail")
13	David	Watson	59	=IF(Mark_awarded>=50,"Pass","Fail")

Nested IFs

This next example illustrates nested IFs. We are going to add another column to our worksheet to give the Grade achieved by each student. We need to use the IF function to check the Total Mark and return the appropriate grade.

* IF a student gets 70% or more the grade is an A.
* IF the student gets 60% to 69% the grade is a B.
* IF the student gets 50% to 59% the grade is a C.
* Less than 50% is a fail.

As we have four possible outcomes (not just a Pass or Fail) we must nest our IF functions to work through the various options.

* Add a new column heading, 'Grade', in the column to the right of the *Result* column.

1 Select the first cell in the *Grade* column.

2 On the **Formulas** tab, click **Logical** in the **Function Library** and select **IF**.

3 In the **Function Arguments** dialog box, enter the condition that you want to be evaluated in the **Logical test** field (Mark_awarded>=70 in this case) and specify the **Value if true** – A (70% and over gets an A).

4 In the **Value if false** field, click **IF** at the top of the **Regularly used functions** list (left end of Formula bar).

5 Complete the next set of conditions and values. Enter the condition that you want to be evaluated in the **Logical test**

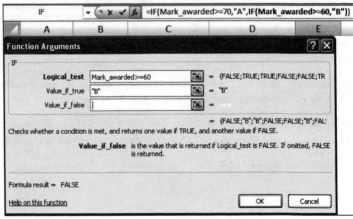

field (Mark_awarded>=60), and specify the **Value if true** – B (60%–69% gets a B grade).

6 In the **Value if false** field, click the **IF** at the top of the Regularly used functions list.

7 Enter the **Logical test** – Mark_awarded>=50.

8 Specify the **Value if true** – C (50%–59% gets a C grade) and the **Value if false** – Fail.

9 Click **OK**.

♦ AutoFill the functions down the column.

	A	B	C	D	E
	E4		fx	"Fail")}}	
1	END OF TERM EXAM RESULTS				
2					
3	Firstname	Surname	Mark awarded	Result	Grade
4	Gill	McLaren	45	Fail	Fail
5	Pauline	Watson	65	Pass	B
6	William	Smith	72	Pass	A
7	Ann	Allan	48	Fail	Fail
8	Andrew	Borthwick	52	Pass	C
9	Peter	Jackson	91	Pass	A
10	Alison	Smith	50	Pass	C
11	Marion	Williamson	49	Fail	Fail
12	Hector	Smith	68	Pass	B
13	David	Watson	59	Pass	C
14					
15					

Alignment / Sales Figures / Southside Film Centre / **Student Results**

Ready   Count: 10

You should get A, B, C and Fail grades as appropriate. If the function does not work as expected, delete it and try again.

In this next example, the IF function is used to work out the amount of discount a customer will get on an order.

♦ If the order is £1000 or over, 10% will be deducted.

♦ If the order is between £750 and £999, 5% will be deducted.

♦ If the order is less than £750, no discount is given.

Enter the basic worksheet as it is displayed here. The empty columns will be completed using functions and formulas.

	A	B	C	D	E	F
1			Sales Orders			
2						
3	Customer Code	Value of Order	Discount	Net Amount	Vat	Total
4	ABC1	£ 1,523.75				
5	DEF2	£ 890.00				
6	GHI3	£ 600.00				
7						

Named ranges have been created for the columns, using the Name Box.

• The Value of order column has been called *VOO*.
• The Discount column has been called *Discount*.
• The Net Amount column has been called *Net_Amount*.
• The VAT column has been called *VAT*.

	A	B	C	D	E	F
1			Sales Orders			
2						
3	Customer Code	Value of Order	Discount	Net Amount	Vat	Total
4	ABC1	£ 1,523.75	£ 152.38	£1,371.38	£239.99	£1,611.37
5	DEF2	£ 890.00	£ 44.50	£ 845.50	£147.96	£ 993.46
6	GHI3	£ 600.00	£ -	£ 600.00	£105.00	£ 705.00
7						
8						

These names have been used in the functions and formulas. The formulas and functions required are shown in the next screenshot.

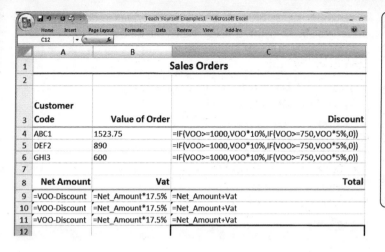

	A	B	C
1		Sales Orders	
2			
3	Customer Code	Value of Order	Discount
4	ABC1	1523.75	=IF(VOO>=1000,VOO*10%,IF(VOO>=750,VOO*5%,0))
5	DEF2	890	=IF(VOO>=1000,VOO*10%,IF(VOO>=750,VOO*5%,0))
6	GHI3	600	=IF(VOO>=1000,VOO*10%,IF(VOO>=750,VOO*5%,0))
7			
8	Net Amount	Vat	Total
9	=VOO-Discount	=Net_Amount*17.5%	=Net_Amount+Vat
10	=VOO-Discount	=Net_Amount*17.5%	=Net_Amount+Vat
11	=VOO-Discount	=Net_Amount*17.5%	=Net_Amount+Vat
12			

AND

The AND function returns a TRUE result if all conditions in the function are met, and a FALSE result if all conditions are not met.

For example, you may manufacture and sell traditional children's wooden toys. Your most popular items are a painted toy box, a rocking horse and building blocks. You want to keep a record of the items that customers buy from you, so that you can see at a glance who has bought at least one of each of these items.

	A	B	C	D	E
1	Customer Purchase Data				
2	Customer	Painted Toy Box	Rocking Horse	Building Blocks	Bought each item
3	Jill Johnston	2	1	2	
4	Peter Jack	0	1	2	
5	Bart Simpson	1	1	4	
6	Ann Black	1	0	1	
7					

You could enter the data into a spreadsheet and use **AND** to return a TRUE value if a customer buys >0 of each item, and FALSE if they don't. In this example, you would create the function in E3 like this:

1 Click the **Logical function** button in the **Function Library** group on the **Formulas** tab.

2 Choose **AND** from the list.

3 In the **Logical1** field, enter B3>0.

4 In the **Logical2** field, enter C3>0.

5 In the **Logical3** field, enter D3>0.

6 Click **OK**.

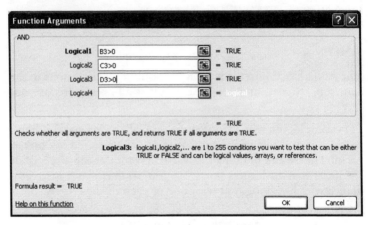

When you copy (AutoFill) the function down the column, you will get a TRUE message where ALL the conditions are met and a FALSE message where they are not.

OR

The OR function will return a TRUE value if *any* condition in the function is met, and FALSE if none are met.

You could add another column to the example used above to identify customers who have bought more than 2 of any item that we sell.

1 Click the **Logical function** button in the **Function Library** group on the **Formulas** tab.

2 Choose OR from the list.

3 In the **Logical1** field, enter B3>2 to check if the value in B3 is greater than 2.

4 In the **Logical2** field, enter C3>2.

5 In the **Logical3** field, enter D3>2.

6 Click **OK**.

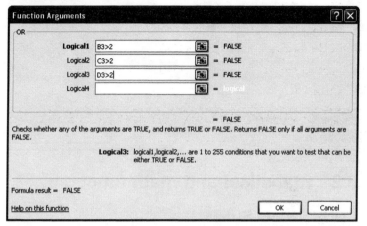

When you copy the function down the column, you will get a TRUE message where *any* condition is met and a FALSE message where none are.

	F3			f_x =OR(B3>2,C3>2,D3>2)	
	A	B	C	D	E	F

1	Customer Purchase Data					
2	Customer	Painted Toy Box	Rocking Horse	Building Blocks	Bought each item	Bought more than 2 of any item
3	Jill Johnston	2	1	2	TRUE	FALSE
4	Peter Jack	0	1	2	FALSE	FALSE
5	Bart Simpson	1	1	4	TRUE	TRUE
6	Ann Black	1	0	1	FALSE	FALSE
7						

You can combine IFs and ANDs and ORs in a variety of ways.

You could use a combination of IF and AND to identify those customers who had bought at least 1 of each item, and display a message saying that they qualify for a free Teddy Bear, or perform a calculation to give a 5% discount. Your **Function Arguments** would look something like the next screenshot – with the AND function *nested* within an IF.

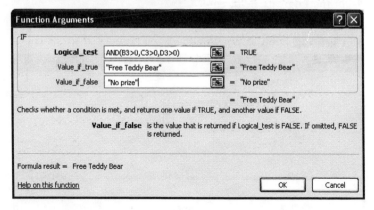

6.2 Statistical and math functions

COUNTIF and SUMIF

COUNTIF looks at a list of values and calculates how many of them satisfy specified criteria. It can be used when you're checking for **one** criterion. The syntax is =COUNTIF(Range,Criteria)

1 Click the **Insert Function** button at the left of the Formula bar (or on the **Formulas** tab).

2 Select the COUNTIF function (you'll find it in the Statistical or All categories).

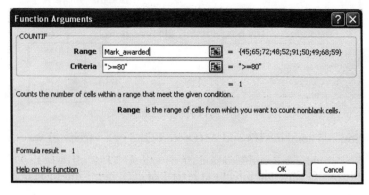

3 Enter the range of cells that you want to be counted in the **Range** field.

4 Specify the criteria that must be met for an entry to be counted in the **Criteria** field.

5 Click **OK**.

The function could be used to count the number of students that obtained specific results in their exams.

	A	B	C	D	E	F	G	H
1			**END OF TERM EXAM RESULTS**					
2								
3	**Firstname**	**Surname**	**Mark awarded**	**Result**	**Grade**			
4	Gill	McLaren	45	Fail	Fail		No of students with	
5	Pauline	Watson	65	Pass	B		>=80	1
6	William	Smith	72	Pass	A			
7	Ann	Allan	48	Fail	Fail		No of students with	
8	Andrew	Borthwick	52	Pass	C		<50	3
9	Peter	Jackson	91	Pass	A			
10	Alison	Smith	50	Pass	C			
11	Marion	Williamson	49	Fail	Fail			
12	Hector	Smith	68	Pass	B			
13	David	Watson	59	Pass	C			

The **SUMIF** function (in the **Math & Trig** category) works in a similar way to COUNTIF, but adds the values together if the condition is met.

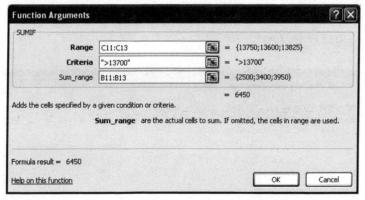

The **Range** is the range of cells you want evaluated.

The **Criteria** specify the conditions you want to check for.

Sum_range is the range of cells to add together. If this is left blank, the cells identified in the Range field will be added.

6.3 Text functions

There are a number of text functions that you may find useful from time to time. They are very easy to use. You could type up a list of names and experiment using the functions discussed.

	Firstname	Surname	Full Name	Full Name in UPPER case	Full Name in LOWER Case	Full Name with Initial Capitals
2	Gill	Mclaren				
3	Peter	Shaw				
4	Kim	Stephen				
5	Andrew	Borthwick				
6	Alison	Peterson				
7	Amanda	Mitchell				
8	Gordon	Williamson				
9	Clare	Stephen				
10	Jack	Williamson				
11	Ann	Shaw				
12	Alison	Anderson				

CONCATENATE

The CONCATENATE function joins text together. In this example it displays the full name in column C.

1 Click the **Text** button in the **Function Library** group on the **Formulas** tab.

2 Select the **Concatenate** function.

3 Enter the cell address that contains the first piece of text required in **Text1.**

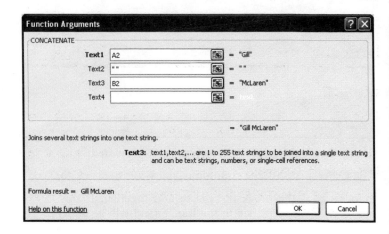

4 Put a space – this could be any character – in **Text2** (in quotation marks). If you don't put in a space, the words will run together.

5 Enter the cell address that contains the next piece of text required in **Text3**.

6 Continue until all text strings have been entered – you can have up to 30 text strings.

7 Click **OK**.

UPPER

UPPER is a case change function. You can use it to change the letters in a text entry to upper case. You could use the UPPER function to display the full name in upper case in Column D.

1 Click the **Text** button in the **Function Library** group on the **Formulas** tab.

2 Select the UPPER function.

3 Enter the cell address that contains the text you want to convert e.g. **C2**.

4 Click **OK**.

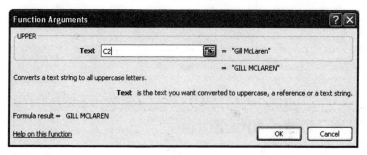

LOWER

LOWER is also a case change function. You can use it to change the letters in a text entry to lower case.

You could use the LOWER function to display the full name in lower case in Column E.

1 Click the **Text** button in the **Function Library** group on the **Formulas** tab.

2 Select the **LOWER** function.

3 Enter the cell address that contains the text you want to convert e.g. **C2**.

4 Click **OK**.

PROPER

PROPER converts a text entry to initial capitals. You could use it to display the name with initial capitals in Column F.

1 Click the **Text** button in the **Function Library** group on the **Formulas** tab.

2 Select the **PROPER** function.

3 Enter the cell address that contains the text you want to convert e.g. **C2**.

4 Click **OK**.

	A	B	C	D	E	F
				Full Name in UPPER case	Full Name in LOWER Case	Full Name with Initial Capitals
1	Firstname	Surname	Full Name			
2	Gill	McLaren	=CONCATENATE(A2," ",B2)	=UPPER(C2)	=LOWER(C2)	=PROPER(C2)
3	Peter	Shaw	=CONCATENATE(A3," ",B3)	=UPPER(C3)	=LOWER(C3)	=PROPER(C3)
4	Kim	Stephen	=CONCATENATE(A4," ",B4)	=UPPER(C4)	=LOWER(C4)	=PROPER(C4)
5	Andrew	Borthwick	=CONCATENATE(A5," ",B5)	=UPPER(C5)	=LOWER(C5)	=PROPER(C5)
6	Alison	Peterson	=CONCATENATE(A6," ",B6)	=UPPER(C6)	=LOWER(C6)	=PROPER(C6)
7	Amanda	Mitchell	=CONCATENATE(A7," ",B7)	=UPPER(C7)	=LOWER(C7)	=PROPER(C7)
8	Gordon	Williamson	=CONCATENATE(A8," ",B8)	=UPPER(C8)	=LOWER(C8)	=PROPER(C8)
9	Clare	Stephen	=CONCATENATE(A9," ",B9)	=UPPER(C9)	=LOWER(C9)	=PROPER(C9)
10	Jack	Williamson	=CONCATENATE(A10," ",B10)	=UPPER(C10)	=LOWER(C10)	=PROPER(C10)
11	Ann	Shaw	=CONCATENATE(A11," ",B11)	=UPPER(C11)	=LOWER(C11)	=PROPER(C11)
12	Alison	Anderson	=CONCATENATE(A12," ",B12)	=UPPER(C12)	=LOWER(C12)	=PROPER(C12)
13						

6.4 Date functions

Date functions allow you to insert the current date and/or time into a cell on your worksheet (or into calculations), and display the date and/or time in a variety of ways.

TODAY()

The TODAY() function enters the date from your computer clock into your worksheet. It's such a regularly used function that most people enter it directly through the keyboard.

To insert the current day:

1 Select a cell in your worksheet.

2 Type in =**TODAY**() – you *must* type in the = and the () to get the function to work.

3 Press [**Enter**].

Or

1 Click the **Date & Time** button in the **Function Library** group on the **Formulas** tab.

2 Choose **Today** from the list.

3 Click **OK**.

NOW()

The NOW() function enters the date and time from your computer clock. Again, it is usually typed in through the keyboard.

To insert the current day:

1 Select a cell in your worksheet.

2 Type in =**NOW**() – you *must* type in the = and the ().

3 Press [**Enter**].

Or

1 Click the **Date & Time** button in the **Function Library** group on the **Formulas** tab.

2 Choose **Now** from the list.

3 Click **OK**.

◆ If the date and/or time are not correct when you use these functions you will need to reset the clock on your computer.

◆ If the NOW() function does not display as a Date and Time, display the **Format Cells** dialog box, choose the **Custom** category on the **Number** tab, and select a Date and Time format.

The values in the cells with the TODAY() or NOW() function in them are volatile. The TODAY() function will be updated automatically. The NOW() function will be updated each time the worksheet is recalculated – click the **Calculate** command button in the **Calculation** group (or press [**F9**]).

DAY, MONTH and YEAR

The **DAY**, **MONTH** and **YEAR** functions can be used to display just the section of the date required. You can use the function to return the portion required from a date entered into a cell in your worksheet, or you can nest the TODAY or NOW function within it.

To return part of a date already in a cell:

1 Select the cell that you want the DAY, MONTH or YEAR displayed in.

2 Click the **Date & Time** command button.

3 Choose DAY, MONTH or YEAR from the function list.

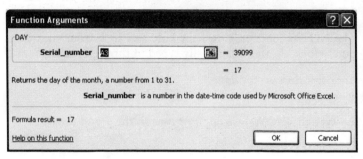

4 Enter the cell address in the **Serial_Number** field.

5 Click **OK**.

To enter part of a date from a TODAY() or NOW() function:

1 Select the cell that you want the DAY, MONTH or YEAR in.

2 Click the **Date & Time** button.

3 Choose DAY, MONTH or YEAR from the function list.

4 Type TODAY() or NOW() in the **Serial_Number** field.

5 Click **OK**.

The TODAY() and NOW() functions are useful when calculating things like age, length of service, or the length of time an item has been in stock.

	A	B	C
1	Employee Name	Start Date	Length of Service (Years)
2	William Smith	34768	=YEAR(TODAY())-YEAR(Start_Date)
3	Joyce Andrews	38169	=YEAR(TODAY())-YEAR(Start_Date)
4			
5	Student Name	Date of Birth	Age (Years)
6	Gill Adams	32091	=YEAR(TODAY())-YEAR(Date_of_Birth)
7	Peter Smith	27473	=YEAR(TODAY())-YEAR(Date_of_Birth)
8			
9	Item	Delivery Date	Time in stock (Days)
10	Chest of Drawers	38986	=TODAY()-Delivery_Date
11	Table	38899	=TODAY()-Delivery_Date
12			

Using Date functions to calculate lengths of time: the formulas…

	A	B	C	D	E
1	Employee Name	Start Date	Length of Service (Years)		
2	William Smith	10/03/1995	11		
3	Joyce Andrews	01/07/2004	2		
4					
5	Student Name	Date of Birth	Age (Years)		
6	Gill Adams	10/11/1987	19		
7	Peter Smith	20/03/1975	31		
8					
9	Item	Delivery Date	Time in stock (Days)		
10	Chest of Drawers	26/09/2006	87		
11	Table	01/07/2006	174		
12					

… and the resulting values.

6.5 Financial functions

Out of the many financial functions in Excel, those dealing with loans and investments are perhaps the ones that are most useful to us all, at a personal if not professional level. Three deal with the repayment of loans (which we all have to handle at some time!), and two are useful when working with savings and investments. The arguments used in these functions are:

pv	the present (original) value of the loan
pmt	the repayment per period
rate	the interest rate per period
nper	the total number of payments

The three functions that can be used with loans are:

=PMT (rate, nper, pv)

calculates the payment each period if the **rate**, **nper** and **pv** are known.

=RATE (nper, pmt, pv)

calculates the interest rate provided the **nper**, **pmt** and **pv** are known.

=PV (rate, nper, pmt)

calculates the loan value provided **rate**, **nper** and **pmt** are known.

Functions that are useful when dealing with investments are:

=FV (rate, nper, pmt)

calculates the final value of saving an amount (**pmt**) for a specific time (**nper**) at a given interest **rate**.

=NPV (rate, value1, value2...)

calculates the net present value of an investment using a comparison discount rate (**rate**) and a series of future income payments from the investment (positive values) and payments to the investment (negative payments). You can have up to 29 value arguments. Basically, if the NPV result is positive, the investment is worth doing.

Have a look at (and experiment with) these examples of how these functions can be used. You'll find other examples (and more information on these functions) in the Help system.

=PMT(rate, nper, pv)

You have decided to extend your house. Your architect estimates that it will cost £20,000. Your bank is prepared to give you a loan for this, at 10% interest per year, over 10 years. What is the monthly repayment on the loan? To work this, you can use the =PMT function. The arguments would be:

=PMT(10%/12, 10*12, 20000)

10%/12 is the monthly interest repayment

10*12 is the number of repayments you will make

20000 is the amount you will borrow

Your monthly repayments would be £264.30.

=RATE (nper, pmt, pv)

What is the interest rate of a 4-year loan for £10,000 with a monthly payment (at the end of the month) of £390?

=RATE (4*12, -390, 10000)

4*12 is the number of repayments

-390 is the amount that you repay each month

10000 is the amount of the loan

The interest rate is 3%.

=PV (rate, nper, pmt)

You need to borrow some money to buy a car. You have worked out your finances, and have calculated that the most you can afford to pay back each month is £250. Your bank is willing to offer you a loan, over 4 years, at 5% interest. How much can you afford to borrow?

=PV(5%/12, 4*12, -250)

5%/12 is the interest rate per month

4*12 is the number of payments over the 4 years

-250 is the amount that you pay each month

The amount you can afford to borrow is £10,855.74.

=FV (rate, nper, pmt)

You inherit £10,000 that is deposited in a savings account that pays 7% annual interest. If you leave the interest in the account and deposit a further £1,000 at the end of each subsequent year, what will the savings account be worth in 10 years' time?

=FV(7%, 10, -1000, -10000)

7% is the interest paid each year

10 is the number of payments

-1000 is the amount that you pay each year

-10000 is the initial amount deposited when you opened the account (the pv)

Your savings account will be worth £33,487.96.

=NPV (rate, value1, value2...)

You are considering investing £20,000 in a venture which will pay you an annual income of £7,200, £8,400 and £10,400 in the next three years. The current rate of interest is 7.5%. What is the NPV of your investment?

=NPV(7.5%, -20000, 7200, 8400, 10400)

7.5% is the interest rate

-20000 is the initial payment (negative value as you paid it in)

7200, 8400, 10400 are the amounts that you receive in the next three years (positive values as it is money you receive)

The NPV of your investment would be £2,174.94.

6.6 Lookup functions

You can locate values in a table using the HLOOKUP (horizontal) or VLOOKUP (vertical) functions.

Use HLOOKUP when your comparison values are located in a row across the top of a table of data, and you want to look along a row to that column.

The format of the function is:

=HLOOKUP(Lookup value, table array, row number)

You can identify the column using cell addresses or column labels.

Use VLOOKUP when your comparison values are located in a column to the left of the data you want to find, and you want to look down a column until the data is located.

=VLOOKUP(Lookup value, table array, column number)

You can identify the row using cell addresses or row labels.

	A	B	C	D	E	F
	E10	▾	fx			
1	Country	Life Expectancy	Population (mills)			
2	France	76	96		HLOOKUP	
3	Gambia	44	0.18		=HLOOKUP("Population (millions)",A1:C10,8)	Population of Portugal
4	Germany	75	77.6		=HLOOKUP("Life Expectancy",A1:C10,6)	Life expectancy in Italy
5	Ireland	78	0.3			
6	Italy	75	57.1		VLOOKUP	
7	Mozambique	47	15.2		=VLOOKUP("Gambia",A1:C10,2)	Life expectancy in Gambia
8	Portugal	74	10.3		=VLOOKUP("Spain",A1:C10,3)	Population of Spain
9	Spain	77	39.1			
10	UK	76	57.1			
11						

LOOKUP formulas...

	A	B	C	D	E	F	G
	E11	▾	fx				
1	Country	Life Expectancy	Population (mills)				
2	France	76	96		HLOOKUP		
3	Gambia	44	0.18		10.3	Population of Portugal	
4	Germany	75	77.6		75	Life expectancy in Italy	
5	Ireland	78	0.3				
6	Italy	75	57.1		VLOOKUP		
7	Mozambique	47	15.2		44	Life expectancy in Gambia	
8	Portugal	74	10.3		39.1	Population of Spain	
9	Spain	77	39.1				
10	UK	76	57.1				

... and their results

6.7 Data tables

A data table is a range of values that can be substituted into a formula.

There are two types of data tables – one-variable (where one value in the formula is substituted) and two-variable (where two values in the formula are substituted).

One-variable data table

In a one-variable data table, the values can be listed down a column or across a row.

In this example, we have a distance of 4,000 miles to travel, and want to work out how long the journey will take. We can use a one-variable data table to show us how long it will take to travel the distance. The time taken depends on the speed at which we travel (the variable). The basic formula to calculate the time it takes will be Distance/Speed.

1 Enter the distance that you need to travel in a cell, eg. **B2**.

2 Enter the variable data (the speeds that you could average each hour) either across one row or down one column, eg. **A5:A8**.

Column-orientated table:

1 Type the formula (**B2/E2**) that refers to the input cell in the row above the first value and one cell to the right of the column of values, e.g. **B4**. Type any additional formulas to the right of the first formula.

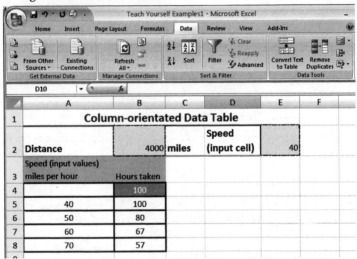

2 Select the range of cells that contain the formulas and values that you want to substitute – A5:B8.

3 On the **Data** tab, click **What-If Analysis** in the **Data Tools** group and select **Data Table** from the options.

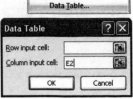

4 Type the cell reference for the input cell in the **Column input cell** box – E2.

5 Click **OK**.

| | E2 | ▼ | fx | 40 | |

	A	B	C	D	E
1	**Column-orientated Data Table**				
2	Distance	4000	miles	Speed (input cell)	40
3	Speed (input values) miles per hour	Hours taken			
4		=B2/E2			
5	40	=TABLE(,E2)			
6	50	=TABLE(,E2)			
7	60	=TABLE(,E2)			
8	70	=TABLE(,E2)			
9					

Row-orientated table:

1 Type the formula in the column to the left of the first value and one cell below the row of values. Type any additional formulas below the first formula.

2 Select the range of cells that contain the formulas and values you want to substitute.

3 On the **Data** tab, click **What-If Analysis** in the **Data Tools** group and select **Data Table** from the options.

4 Type the cell reference for the input cell in the **Row input cell** box.

Two-variable data table

A two-variable input table is very similar, but with a row and a column input value. You could create a two-variable input table to calculate the 'times tables' from 1 to 12.

1 Enter the formula that refers to the two input cells in a cell on the worksheet (in B4 in this example).

2 Enter one list of input values in the same column, below the formula.

3 Enter the second list of input values in the same row, to the right of the formula.

4 Select the range of cells that contains the formula and both the row and column of values (B4:N16).

5 On the **Data** tab, click **What-If Analysis** in the **Data Tools** group and select **Data Table** from the options.

6 In the **Row input cell** box, enter the reference to the input cell for the input values in the row.

7 In the **Column input cell** box, enter the reference to the input cell for the input values in the column.

8 Click **OK**.

◆ Go to one-variable and two-variable data tables in Help for more information.

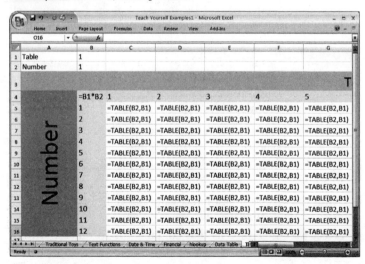

	A	B	C	D	E	F	G	H	I	J	K	L	M	N
1	Table	1												
2	Number	1												
3							Table							
4		1	1	2	3	4	5	6	7	8	9	10	11	12
5		1	1	2	3	4	5	6	7	8	9	10	11	12
6		2	2	4	6	8	10	12	14	16	18	20	22	24
7		3	3	6	9	12	15	18	21	24	27	30	33	36
8		4	4	8	12	16	20	24	28	32	36	40	44	48
9		5	5	10	15	20	25	30	35	40	45	50	55	60
10		6	6	12	18	24	30	36	42	48	54	60	66	72
11		7	7	14	21	28	35	42	49	56	63	70	77	84
12		8	8	16	24	32	40	48	56	64	72	80	88	96
13		9	9	18	27	36	45	54	63	72	81	90	99	108
14		10	10	20	30	40	50	60	70	80	90	100	110	120
15		11	11	22	33	44	55	66	77	88	99	110	121	132
16		12	12	24	36	48	60	72	84	96	108	120	132	144
17														

(Column A, rows 6–16: "Number")

The completed data table, showing values...

	A	B	C	D	E	F	G
	O16						
1	Table	1					
2	Number	1					
3							T
4		=B1*B2	1	2	3	4	5
5		1	=TABLE(B2,B1)	=TABLE(B2,B1)	=TABLE(B2,B1)	=TABLE(B2,B1)	=TABLE(B2,B1)
6		2	=TABLE(B2,B1)	=TABLE(B2,B1)	=TABLE(B2,B1)	=TABLE(B2,B1)	=TABLE(B2,B1)
7		3	=TABLE(B2,B1)	=TABLE(B2,B1)	=TABLE(B2,B1)	=TABLE(B2,B1)	=TABLE(B2,B1)
8		4	=TABLE(B2,B1)	=TABLE(B2,B1)	=TABLE(B2,B1)	=TABLE(B2,B1)	=TABLE(B2,B1)
9		5	=TABLE(B2,B1)	=TABLE(B2,B1)	=TABLE(B2,B1)	=TABLE(B2,B1)	=TABLE(B2,B1)
10		6	=TABLE(B2,B1)	=TABLE(B2,B1)	=TABLE(B2,B1)	=TABLE(B2,B1)	=TABLE(B2,B1)
11		7	=TABLE(B2,B1)	=TABLE(B2,B1)	=TABLE(B2,B1)	=TABLE(B2,B1)	=TABLE(B2,B1)
12		8	=TABLE(B2,B1)	=TABLE(B2,B1)	=TABLE(B2,B1)	=TABLE(B2,B1)	=TABLE(B2,B1)
13		9	=TABLE(B2,B1)	=TABLE(B2,B1)	=TABLE(B2,B1)	=TABLE(B2,B1)	=TABLE(B2,B1)
14		10	=TABLE(B2,B1)	=TABLE(B2,B1)	=TABLE(B2,B1)	=TABLE(B2,B1)	=TABLE(B2,B1)
15		11	=TABLE(B2,B1)	=TABLE(B2,B1)	=TABLE(B2,B1)	=TABLE(B2,B1)	=TABLE(B2,B1)
16		12	=TABLE(B2,B1)	=TABLE(B2,B1)	=TABLE(B2,B1)	=TABLE(B2,B1)	=TABLE(B2,B1)

Teach Yourself Examples1 - Microsoft Excel

Home   Insert   Page Layout   Formulas   Data   Review   View   Add-Ins

(Column A, rows 6–16: "Number")

Traditional Toys / Text Functions / Date & Time / Financial / Hlookup / Data Table / T

Ready

... and showing formulas

6.8 Goal Seek

Another useful What-If function is Goal Seek. This allows you to specify the goal you are seeking, and get Excel to work out the value of a given source cell to enable you to reach your goal. The cell whose value you are changing – in our example the *Payment* value – must contain a formula.

Let's say you had decided to purchase a property, and you had worked out that you could afford to pay £750 per month in a mortgage. You have decided on a fixed rate mortgage, and the interest rate is 3%. You want to know how much you can borrow. Excel can help you work this out. Enter the data that you know into a worksheet (the *Loan Amount* is the unknown in this example, so enter any value initially). The *Payment* cell contains the formula =PMT(B2/12,B3,B1) – this will be the cell that we want to change during the Goal Seek.

	A	B	C	D	E
	B4	▾	f_x =PMT(B2/12,B3,B1)		
1	Loan Amount	£ 100,000.00	amount borrowed		
2	Interest Rate	3%	fixed rate		
3	Period	180	payments over 15 years		
4	Payment	-£690.58	monthly payment		

We want to work out the *Loan* value, by setting the *Payment* cell value to £750.

1 On the **Data** tab, click **What-If Analysis** in the **Data Tools** group and select **Goal Seek...** from the options.

2 In the **Goal Seek** dialog box, set the conditions. Here we want to set the payment in B4 to –750 (minus because we are paying out), by changing the loan amount in cell B1.

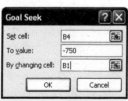

3 Click **OK**.

4 At the **Goal Seek Solution** dialog box, your setting will be confirmed, and you will see the result on your worksheet – £108,604.10.

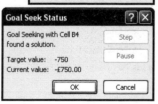

5 Click **OK** to close the dialog box and update the worksheet.

You might decide that this is not enough to purchase a property in your chosen area, and your sister offers to join forces with you so that you can both get onto the property ladder. Between you, you can afford to payback £1,400 per month. If you check it out you should find that you can afford to borrow £202,707.66 between you.

6.9 Scenarios

A scenario is a named set of values that can be applied to a set of selected cells in your workbook. They are used when you want to set up a model where you can quickly substitute the various inputs so that you can compare the solutions. They are useful in 'What-If' situations, where you can set up several named inputs and apply them to you worksheet to help identify best and worst cases.

Let's say you wanted to perform some calculations to work out the monthly repayments that you would have to make on a loan. You are considering three options.

	Amount of loan	Interest rate	Payback period
Option 1	£20,000	7%	5 years
Option 2	£25,000	7%	8 years
Option 3	£30,000	10%	12 years

You could set up each option as a scenario.

1 Set up your worksheet to show the Option 1 payments and input the formula required.

B7		f_x	=PMT(Interest_Rate/12,Period*12,Loan)		
	A	B	C	D	E
1	**Loan repayment calculations**				
2					
3	Loan	£20,000.00			
4	Interest Rate	7%	per annum		
5	Period	5	years		
6					
7	Payment	-£396.02			
8					

2 On the **Data** tab, click **What-If Analysis** in the **Data Tools** group and select **Scenario Manager...** from the options.

3 At the **Scenario Manager** dialog box click **Add...**

4 Give the scenario a name, e.g. Option 1.

5 Specify the cells that will change when you show the various scenarios, e.g. B3:B5 and click **OK**.

6 Type the values in for Option 1 and click **Add**.

7 Repeat steps 4–6 for Option 2 and 3.

8 Click **OK**.

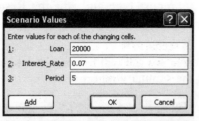

The scenarios will be listed in the Scenario Manager dialog box. If a scenario is wrong or no longer required, you can edit or delete it from this dialog box.

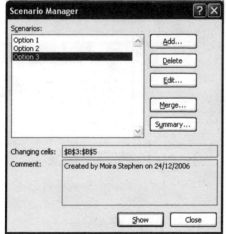

To see the repayment options, select an option and click **Show** – the values on your worksheet will be substituted by those in the scenario.

When you show each scenario in turn, you can see the outcome of applying that scenario only. If you wish to see the outcomes of all the scenarios at once (which makes it easier to compare them) you must create a scenario summary.

To create a scenario summary:

1 On the **Data** tab, click **What-If Analysis** in the **Data Tools** group and select **Scenario Manager...**

2 At the **Scenario Manager** dialog box click **Summary...**

3 Choose **Scenario summary** as the report type and edit the **Result cells** field if necessary.

4 Click **OK**.

A new sheet will be created showing the summary report.

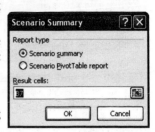

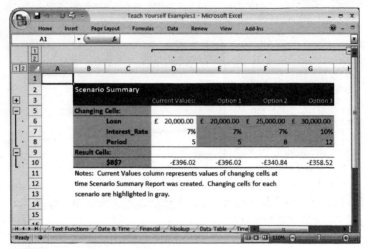

6.10 PivotTable

There may be times when you want to create a report that summarizes the data held in a worksheet. You might want to perform some calculations on the summarized data, or filter it to display specific data from the list. PivotTables can be used in this situation. They are interactive tables that allow you to summarize large amounts of data.

A PivotTable has four areas – page, column, row and data. The page, column and row areas show the data that you have added to the PivotTable – they act as labels for the data that you are summarizing. They are also used to filter the data that you add.

The data area is where the summary result calculations are performed and displayed. Each item in the data area must have a function associated with it – sum, average, count, etc.

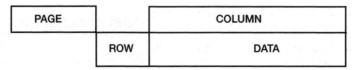

PAGE	COLUMN	
	ROW	DATA

You don't *have* to have an item in the page, column or row area, but you *must* have something in the data area (you have to be summarizing something!).

In this example we've used Excel to record details of customer orders. We then go on to summarize this data using a PivotTable. We want to be able to:

◆ Display the order data by town.

◆ Filter the data to show the order data from each customer.

◆ Calculate totals for the number of each item purchased.

To create a PivotTable:

1 Click anywhere inside the list of data for which you want to create a PivotTable.

2 On the **Insert** tab, click the **PivotTable** command button in the **Tables** group.

3 Choose the **Select a table or range** option, check the cell range and edit if necessary.

4 Specify where you want the PivotTable displayed.

5 Click **OK**.

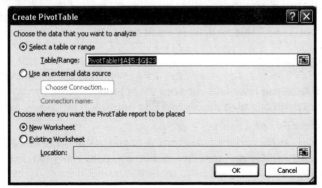

The PivotTable is created, and the PivotTable Tools are displayed in the Ribbon, with an Options tab and a Design tab.

To layout your data:

1 Select the fields that you want to appear in the PivotTable.

2 Drag and drop the fields from one report area to another to see how this affects the layout of your chart.

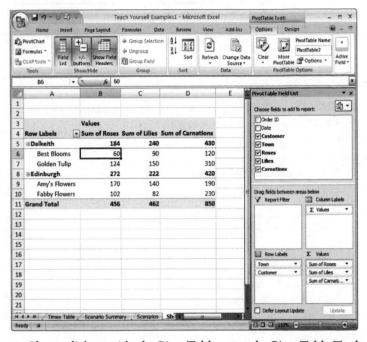

• If you click outside the PivotTable area, the PivotTable Tools and the Field List pane disappear – just click anywhere within the PivotTable to display them again.

Show/Hide

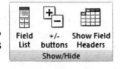

• Once you have laid out your PivotTable, experiment with the Show/Hide buttons to see their effect.

• Try moving the fields from one area to another to see the effect it has on your PivotTable, e.g. drag the Town into the Report Filter area.

PivotTable Options

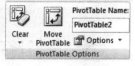

- To clear your PivotTable (so you can start again!) – click the **Clear** button in the **PivotTable Options** group and then choose **Clear All**.

- To name your PivotTable, edit the default name in the **PivotTable Options** group.

- To move your PivotTable, click the **Move PivotTable** button in the **PivotTable Options** group. You can move it to a new worksheet, or to another location in the existing sheet.

Data

- When the source data is updated, click the **Refresh** button in the Data group to update the data in your PivotTable.

- If you wish to change or edit the data source, use the **Change Data Source** button to open a dialog box where you can adjust the source range.

To change the design of your PivotTable:

- Display the **Design** tab in the **Pivot Table** tools.

Experiment with the Layout, PivotTable Style Options and PivotTable Styles to see what options are available to you.

6.11 Consolidating data

Consolidation is used to combine values from multiple ranges into one new range, while processing the values using an Excel function e.g. sum, count, average, minimum.

There are various ways of consolidating your data, but the most commonly used options are discussed here.

	A	B	C	D	E
1	Branch Sales Figures				
2		January - April			
3		Tyres	Exhausts	Accessories	Total
4	Aberdeen				£ -
5	Dunfermline				£ -
6	Dundee				£ -
7	Edinburgh				£ -
8	Glasgow				£ -
9	Inverness				£ -
10	Perth				£ -
11	Total	£ -	£ -	£ -	
12					

Consolidate by position

You could use this method if the source data and the destination data are laid out in the same way. This example consolidates data from four separate worksheets – January, February, March and April. These sheets contain sales data for company branches. The data for each month has the same layout, as has the worksheet being used to consolidate the data.

1 Select the range of cells that the source data will be consolidated into.

2 Click the **Consolidate** button in the **Data Tools** group on the **Data** tab.

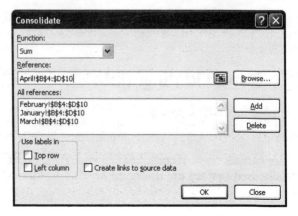

3 Select the function from the **Function** list.

4 Enter the first cell range into the **Reference** field.

5 Click **Add**.

6 Repeat steps 4 and 5 for each range you wish to add.

7 Select the **Create links to source data** checkbox if you want the consolidated data to be updated any time the source data changes.

8 Click **OK**.

• If the **Create links** checkbox is selected, the outline pane is open so you can expand and collapse the level of detail displayed as required.

		A	B	C	D	E
	1			Branch Sales Figures		
	2			January - April		
	3		Tyres	Exhausts	Accessories	Total
+	8	Aberdeen	£ 11,100.00	£ 11,800.00	£ 9,900.00	£32,800.00
+	13	Dunfermline	£ 12,900.00	£ 10,400.00	£ 15,500.00	£38,800.00
+	18	Dundee	£ 13,000.00	£ 10,600.00	£ 11,200.00	£34,800.00
+	23	Edinburgh	£ 20,600.00	£ 19,600.00	£ 21,000.00	£61,200.00
+	28	Glasgow	£ 20,500.00	£ 21,000.00	£ 18,500.00	£60,000.00
+	33	Inverness	£ 13,500.00	£ 13,000.00	£ 13,500.00	£40,000.00
+	38	Perth	£ 12,700.00	£ 9,200.00	£ 18,500.00	£40,400.00
	39	Total	£ 197,500.00	£ 179,400.00	£ 206,300.00	
	40					

Consolidate by formula

You could also consolidate your data by using a formula that references cells in different worksheets. The data may be in different cells on each sheet, or in the same cell in each sheet.

It is not necessary to have the consolidated data presented using the same layout as the source data.

To enter the formula or function:

1 Select the cell that will contain the formula or function.

2 Type in the formula or function (or use Insert Function).

• If the cells are on separate worksheets you can either click on the worksheet tab then click on the cell to enter its location,

or type the sheet name followed by the cell address, e.g. January!B4. Note the '!' after the sheet name.

+ When referencing the same address in a set of sheets you can enter the references as a range, e.g. =SUM(January:April!B4) to indicate it is cell B4 in the worksheets from January to April.

Summary

In this chapter we have introduced:

+ Logical functions – IF, AND, OR

+ Statistical and math functions – COUNTIF and SUMIF

+ Text functions – concatenate, upper, lower, proper

+ Date functions – today, now, day, month and year

+ Financial functions that are used when dealing with loans and investments

+ Lookup functions – HLookup and VLookup

+ What-If Analysis tools – data tables, Goal Seek and scenarios

+ PivotTables

+ Consolidating data.

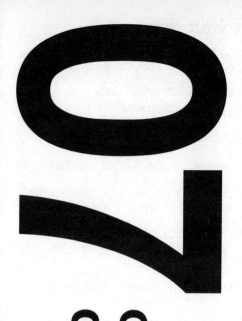

07

charting and drawing

In this chapter you will learn:

- how to produce charts from your data
- about printing charts
- how to add special effects to your charts
- about Shapes

7.1 Preparing your data

Excel can create charts – bar graphs, line graphs, pie charts, scatter diagrams, etc. – from the data in your worksheet.

You can create your chart on the same worksheet as the data on which the chart is built (an embedded chart), or on a separate chart sheet.

* *Ideally* the data should be in adjacent cells.

* If there are blank rows or columns within the data to be charted, remove these before you try to chart it.

To chart data that is not in adjacent cells:

1 Select the first group of cells you want to chart.

2 Hold down [Ctrl] while you click and drag over the other groups you want to include in your chart.

* When the non-adjacent cells are selected, the areas *must* be able to combine to form a rectangle.

Depending on the type of data you are charting, you must ensure that the data is laid out correctly on your worksheet if you hope to chart it successfully. See 'How to arrange data for specific chart types' in 'Create a chart' in the online Help.

7.2 Creating a chart

To create a chart:

1 Select the cells you want to create a chart from.

2 On the **Insert** tab, in the **Charts** group, click the Chart Type button, then click on the subtype you want to use.

Or

3 Click **All Chart Types** at the bottom of the list to display the **Create Chart** dialog box, where all chart types and subtypes are located. Select the chart type and click **OK**.

* The resulting chart is embedded within the worksheet that contains the source data.

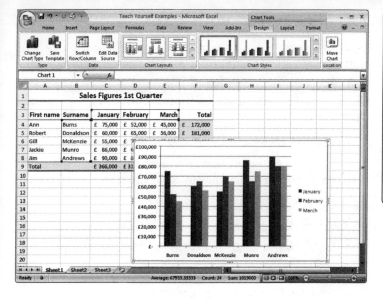

Move, resize and delete charts

If you want to move, resize or delete a chart that is an object on a worksheet, you must select the chart first.

To move the chart:

1 Select the chart.

2 Point to the edge of the chart – the mouse pointer changes to a 4-headed arrow when you are in the correct place.

3 Drag and drop the chart in its new location.

To resize the chart:

1 Select the chart.

2 Point to one of the handles in the corner or along the edge of the chart – the mouse pointer changes to a 2-headed arrow when you are in the correct place.

3 Click and drag to resize the chart.

To delete the chart:

1 Select the chart.

2 Press [**Delete**] on your keyboard.

When a chart is selected Chart Tools appear on the Ribbon. There are three tabs – Design, Layout and Format.

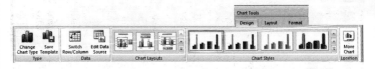

* If you click outside the Chart area, the Chart Tools disappear. Click within the Chart area again and they reappear.

If you don't want your chart embedded in the worksheet that contains its source data, you can easily move it.

To move a chart to a new location:

1 Select the **Design** tab from the **Chart Tools**.

2 Click the **Move Chart** button in the Location group.

3 Select the location.

4 Click **OK**.

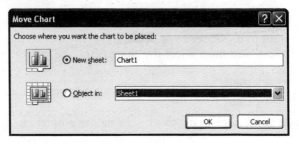

If your chart doesn't look the way you expected, and you think a different chart type would be better, you can change the type at any time.

To change the chart type:

1 Click the **Change Chart Type** button in the Type group on the **Design** tab.

2 Select the type and subtype.

3 Click **OK**.

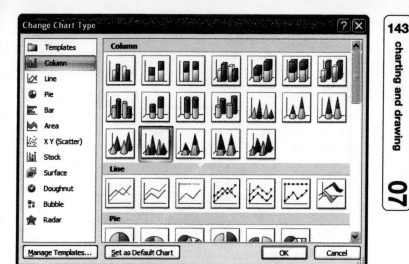

7.3 Adjusting your source data

You can edit the data series for a chart by:

* Editing the range of source data for the whole chart.
* Selecting a new range of source data for the whole chart.
* Editing the ranges that affect the legend entries (series).
* Editing the ranges that affect the horizontal axis labels (categories).
* Rearranging the legend entries.
* Switching the legend entries and horizontal axis labels.

Display the Edit Data Source dialog box to change the cell references of the source data.

1 Click the **Select Data** button in the **Data** group.

To edit the range of chart data, or specify a new range:

2 Amend the **Chart Data Range**.

To amend the legend entries:

3 Select the entry.

4 Click **Edit**.

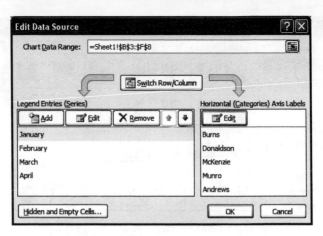

5 At the **Edit Series** dialog box amend the cell address that iden-
tifies the Series name and/or values and click **OK**.

6 If you wish to rearrange the series, select the item you wish
to move and click the **Move up** and **Move down** buttons in
the **Edit Data Source** dialog box.

♦ You can also **Add** new legend entries and **Remove** existing
ones from this dialog box (but this is also done automatically if you adjust the **Chart Data Range** field).

To amend the horizontal axis labels (categories):

7 Click the **Edit** button and adjust the range of source cells in
the Axis Labels dialog box.

8 Click **OK**.

To switch the data:

♦ Click the **Switch Row/Column** button in the **Data** group on
the **Design** tab.

Or

♦ Click **Switch Row/Column** in the **Edit Data Source** dialog
box.

7.4 Chart styles and layouts

Excel has a variety of chart layout and styles that you can use to
quickly adjust and format your chart.

Chart Style

The chart styles give you access to a wide range of carefully colour-coordinated options that can be applied to your chart.

To change the chart style:

1 Select your chart.

2 Scroll through the **Chart Style** options on the **Design** tab of the Chart Tools.

Or

• Click the **More** button at the bottom right of the **Chart Style** group to display the chart styles gallery.

3 Select the one you want to use.

Chart Layout

The layout affects the inclusion and positioning of objects like the chart heading, legend, data table, axis labels, etc.

The quickest way to include/exclude objects from your chart is to use one of the predefined chart layouts.

1 Select your chart.

2 Scroll through the **Chart Lay-out** options on the **Design** tab of the Chart tools.

Or

• Click the **More** button on the **Chart Layout** group to display the layout gallery.

3 Select one.

If you wish, you can customize any object within your chart – the chart title, axis titles, legend.

To delete a chart object:

1 Right-click on it.
2 Select **Delete** from the menu.

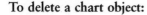

Delete
Reset to Match Style
Change Chart Type...
Edit Data Source...
3-D View...
Format Legend...

To format a chart object:

1 Right-click on the object.
2 Left-click on the **Format Chart Area.../Title.../Data Series...** option (depending on what you right-click on).
3 Explore the dialog box, selecting the options required.
4 Click **OK**.

Chart titles and axis labels

These areas are text boxes, and initially contain default text – chart title in the title area and axis title along each axis.

To replace the default text:

1 Click once on the label to select it.
2 Click on it a second time to place the insertion point in it.
3 Delete the default text.
4 Type in your label.
5 Click outside the title or label area – anywhere on the chart.

Chart Layout options

You can switch individual objects on and off using the buttons in the Labels, Axes and Background groups of the Layout tab, or reposition objects that have been displayed by applying one of the standard layouts.

• The **Labels** group includes the Chart Headings, Axis Titles, Legend, Data Labels and Data Table.

• The **Axes** group includes the Axes and the Gridlines.

- The **Background** group includes the Plot Area (2-D charts), Chart Wall, Chart Floor and 3D View (3-D charts).

To display an object or change its position:

1 Click the object's button.

2 Select the position required.

To remove an object:

1 Click the object's button.

2 Select **None**.

To adjust the format of an object:

1 Click the object's button.

2 Select **More Options...** and explore the dialog box.

3 Select the options and click **OK**.

Some objects have many more options than others. Walls, floors and plot areas have fill colours and fill effects. Lines have styles, colours and widths. The best idea is to explore and experiment – some options will appeal to you, others will not. But don't overdo things! The purpose of your chart will be to clearly and effectively present your data – not demonstrate every Excel chart formatting option!

7.5 More formatting options

The **Formatting** tab offers even more formatting options.

The **Current Selection** group gives you:

- **Format Selection** which opens the **Format** dialog box for the object selected.

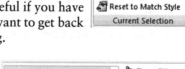

- **Reset to Match Style** – useful if you have been experimenting and want to get back to the original formatting.

The **Shape Styles** group gives access to formatting options that affect the fill, outline and shape of the current selection.

◆ Select the options required from the buttons in the group, or click the **Format Shape** dialog launcher in the bottom right corner of the group to open the dialog box, giving access to all the options for the selected object.

7.6 Default chart

The default chart in Excel is a 2-D column chart.

To quickly produce the default chart:

1 Select the data you wish to chart.

2 Press [F11].

The chart will be displayed in a separate chart sheet, and you can use the Chart Tools to format it as you wish.

If you don't use 2-D column charts very often, you can change the default chart type.

To change the default chart type:

1 Display the **Create Chart** dialog box.

2 Select the chart type and subtype to set as the default.

3 Click the **Set as Default Chart** button.

4 Click **Cancel** to exit the dialog box without creating a chart, or **OK** to create a chart.

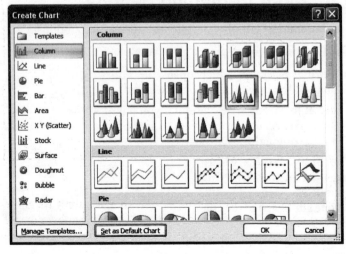

7.7 Special effects

One of the best ways to find out about the charting capabilities is to experiment. However, here are some tips and pointers if you want to get that little bit more from your charts!

Value axis scale

By default, the value axis starts at 0. If you don't have any small values to plot, e.g. if they all are 100,000 and over, this results in a large dead area at the bottom of your chart. To get rid of this, set an appropriate minimum value for the axis.

1 Right-click on the value axis and choose **Format Axis**.

2 In the **Axis** Options, set the minimum value for the axis.

3 Click **Close**.

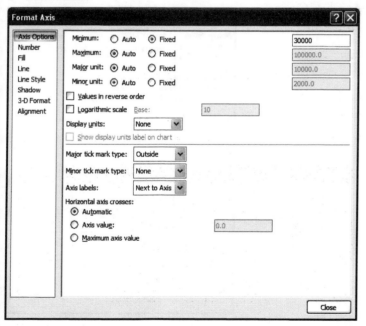

Display units

This is another axis formatting option that is useful for large numbers on the value axis. You can opt to show the units rounded to hundreds, thousands, tens of thousands, hundreds of thousands, millions, tens of millions, hundreds of millions, billions or trillions!

• Explore the other options in this dialog box to see if they would improve your charts.

Overlaps and gap widths

The spacing between each bar or column on a chart is called the overlap. The space between each group of bars or columns is the gap width. You can adjust these settings from the Format Data Series dialog box.

1 Right-click on any data series.

2 Choose **Format Data Series...** from the pop-up menu.

3 Set the **Overlap** and/or **Gap** settings as required.

4 Click **Close**.

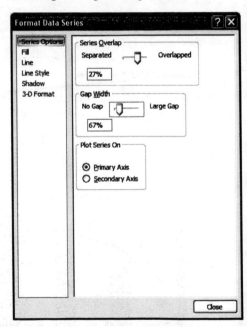

Picture or Texture Fill

The Fill options for a data series include **Picture** or **Texture Fill**. The Picture can be from a file, Clipboard or Clipart.

1 In the **Fill** options, select **Picture** or **Texture** fill.

2 Click:

 File... to use a
picture file.

Clipboard to paste
in an image you
have copied to the
clipboard.

ClipArt... to search
for a suitable piece
of ClipArt.

3 Locate your file/
clipart image and
insert it.

4 Close the dialog
box.

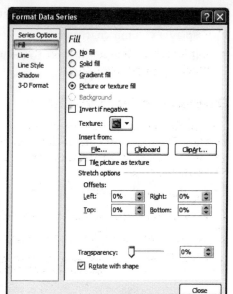

Combined charts

You can customize charts further by combining some chart typed
(you can't combine all types – experiment with them).

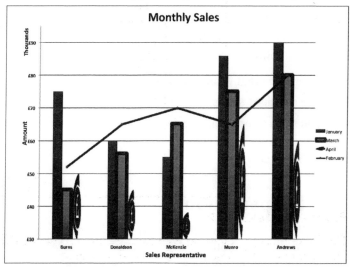

A combined bar and line chart

To combine a column chart with a line chart:

1 Display a column chart in 2-D.

2 Select the series that you wish to display as a line.

3 Click **Change Chart Type** on the **Design** tab.

4 Choose **Line,** then the subtype from the **Chart type** list.

5 Close the dialog box.

6 Format the line as you wish.

7.8 Printing your chart

You can print your chart with or without the data on which it is based. If it is an object in a worksheet you have several print options. Check it through Print Preview before you print.

To print the chart and all of the data on the worksheet:

◆ Print the worksheet as normal (i.e. without selecting the chart).

To get a printout of the chart only:

◆ Select the chart on the worksheet, then print.

To print the chart, plus its data, but no other data:

1 Select the chart.

2 Choose a layout that displays the data table.

3 Print out with the chart selected.

To print a chart that is on a separate chart sheet:

1 Select the chart sheet.

◆ If you want to print out the data, choose a layout with a data table.

2 Print as usual.

7.9 Shapes buttons

Use the Shapes buttons to add effects to your charts and data, e.g. you could draw an arrow, with a message attached, pointing to an object within your chart.

- The **Shapes** are on the **Insert** tab on the Ribbon.

The **Recently used shapes** are displayed initially, but you can use the scroll arrows to move through the various categories of shape, or click the **More** button to display the shapes gallery.

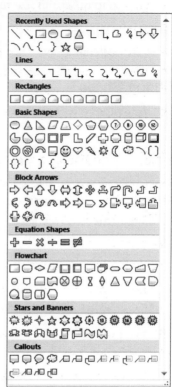

To draw a shape:

1 Click the shape's button.

2 Click and drag on your worksheet to draw the shape.

- For a perfect square or circle, select the **Rectangle** or **Oval** button, and hold down [**Shift**] as you click and drag.

Drawing Tools

When you select a drawing shape, the Drawing Tools appear in the Ribbon. If no shape is selected, the Drawing Tools disappear again.

You can use the buttons on the **Format** tab to format the shapes that you draw. To format your object in any way, you must select it first. Deselect it when you have finished.

To move or resize your shape:

- Click and drag within the object to move it.
- Click and drag a handle to resize the object.

If your shape must be a specific size, you can use the buttons in the **Size** group to set the size required.

To delete a shape:

• Press [Delete].

Shape Styles

Use the Shape Styles buttons to select a different formatting style for your shape.

• **Shape Fill** gives access to all the fill options available for an object, e.g. colour, picture, gradient or texture.

• **Shape Outline** gives access to the line formatting options for the outline, e.g. colour, weight, dashes and arrows.

• **Shape Effects** gives access to a range of preset and fully customizable 3-D and shadow effects for your shape.

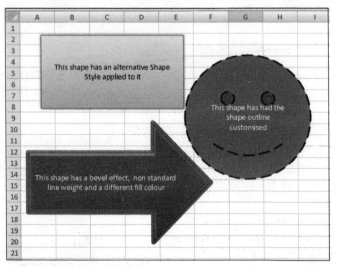

Adding text

To add text to a shape:

1 Right-click on the shape.

2 Select **Edit Text**.

3 Enter the text (or edit existing text).

If you wish to add free text to a worksheet or chart (not within a shape or cell or as a chart object), you can use a text box. A text box can be positioned anywhere on a worksheet or chart.

To insert a text box:

1 Click the **Text box** button on the **Insert** tab, in the **Text** group.

Or

Click the **Text box** 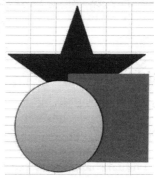 button in the **Insert Shapes** group on the **Format** tab of the Drawing Tools.

2 Drag on your worksheet or chart to draw a rectangle where you want your text box to be.

3 Type in your text.

4 Click outside your text box.

A text box can be resized, moved, formatted or deleted like any other shape.

7.10 Some more options

You can create some interesting effects using shapes, particularly if you layer and group them, or rotate or flip them.

Bring Forward, Send Backward

When you draw your shapes, they are placed in layers on your worksheet. The first shape is on the lowest layer, the next one is on a layer above, the third shape on another layer above that, and so on.

If you move your shapes so that they overlap each other a little you will see this layering effect.

You can move a shape from one layer to another using the **Bring Forward/ Send Backward** commands. These are located in the **Arrange** group on the **Format** tab of the Drawing Tools.

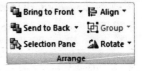

Bring to Front

Click the arrow beside the **Bring to Front** button to display the options:

- **Bring Forward** moves a shape forward one layer at a time.
- **Bring to Front** moves the shape to the top.

Send to Back

Click the arrow beside the **Send to Back** button to display the options:

- **Send Backwards** moves a shape back one layer at a time.
- **Send to Back** moves the shape to the bottom of the pile.

The same shapes after resizing and reordering using the Bring to Front/Send to Back options.

Grouping

If you create an image by layering several shapes, you will find it easier to manage the final image if you group the shapes together. Once the shapes are grouped they can be moved and resized as one object. You can always ungroup the objects again if you wish to edit each shape individually again.

To group shapes:

1 Select the shapes – select the first shape, then hold down [**Shift**] and click on each of the other shapes.

2 Click the **Group** button in the **Arrange** group and then click **Group** in the options.

The shapes are grouped together into one object and can then be resized, moved or deleted as one. If you need to work on an individual shape again, you must ungroup the object again.

To ungroup your shapes:

1 Select the grouped shape.

2 Click the **Group** button and select **Ungroup** from the list.

3 Edit the shapes as necessary.

To regroup the shapes that have been ungrouped:

1 Click the drop-down arrow to the right of the **Group** tool.

2 Choose **Regroup**.

Selection and Visibility pane

As an alternative to using the Select, Bring Forward/Send Backward commands, you could use the **Selection and Visibility pane**.

To switch the pane off and on:

♦ Click the **Selection Pane** button in the **Arrange** group.

To select a shape using the pane:

♦ Click on the shape name in the list.

To show or hide an individual shape:

♦ Click the eye icon to the right of the shape name.

To show or hide all shapes on a sheet:

♦ Click the **Show All** or **Hide All** buttons at the bottom of the pane.

To change the layer each shape is on:

1 Select the shape.

2 Use the **Re-order** buttons at the bottom of the pane.

To delete a shape:

1 Select it in the pane.

2 Press [**Delete**].

Show/Hide shape

Rotate and Flip

Shapes can be rotated left or right 90°, or freely through any angle, or flipped horizontally or vertically.

To rotate a shape:

1 Select the shape.

2 Choose the rotate option from the **Rotate** button in the **Arrange** group.

Summary

This chapter has considered the powerful charting and drawing options available in Excel. We have discussed:

♦ Preparing your data for charting

♦ Creating a chart

♦ Adjusting source data

♦ Chart styles and layout

♦ Formatting options that apply to charts

♦ Printing your chart

♦ Setting your default chart

♦ Special effects

♦ Drawing and manipulating shapes.

08

styles and templates

In this chapter you will learn:

- how to use, create and edit styles
- about workbook, worksheet and chart templates

8.1 Styles

We looked at using standard Excel styles to format worksheets in Chapter 3. We will look at the options available to you when creating and working with your own styles here.

To create your own style, either:

1 Format a cell with the attributes you want to add to a style, e.g. font size, colour, cell colour.

2 Select the cell and click **Cell Styles,** then **New Cell Style...**

3 Give your style a name.

4 Ensure that all the checkboxes are ticked so that the style picks up the formats for the style from the selected cell.

5 Click **OK**.

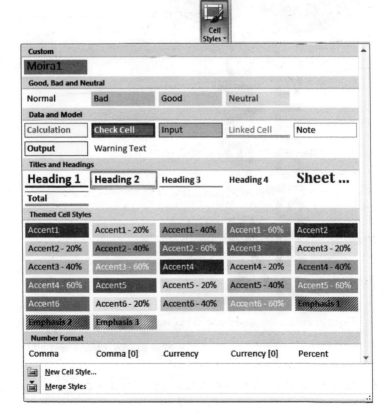

Your style will now appear in the **Cell** list, so you can apply it to any other cells as required.

Or

1 Select any cell and click **Cell Styles**, then **New Cell Style...**

2 Give your style a name.

3 Ensure that all the checkboxes are cleared (unless the cell has an attribute that you wish to include in the style).

4 Click **Format** and format as required using the dialog box.

5 Click **OK**.

To rename or edit a style:

1 Click **Cell Styles** to display the styles.

2 Right-click on the style you wish to change.

3 Click **Modify...**

4 Make your changes – change the name or any of the formatting options.

5 Click **OK**.

Moira...
Apply
Modify...
Duplicate...
Delete
Add Gallery to Quick Access Toolbar

To delete a style:

1 Click **Cell Styles** to display the styles.

2 Right-click on the one you wish to delete.

3 Click on **Delete**.

The style will be removed, and any cells that were formatted with it will revert to the Normal style. If the style's formatting remains applied to the cell, it will be because the cell had been formatted by setting options, not by applying a style – you probably created the style by selecting the options applied to the cell.

To duplicate a style:

1 Click **Cell Styles** to display the styles.

2 Right-click on the style you wish to copy.

3 Click on **Duplicate**.

• A copy of the style will be created.

4 Rename and/or adjust the formatting as required.

5 Click **OK**.

* To give your worksheets a professional look quickly and easily, use styles to format your cells.

8.2 Workbook templates

A template is a design on which a workbook or worksheet is based. It includes things like standard text, formatting and formulas – so all you have to do is add your data. Up until now, your workbooks have been based on the default template – Blank Workbook. This is the one used to create a new workbook when you start Excel.

If you explore the New Workbook dialog box, you will find that there are many templates to choose from.

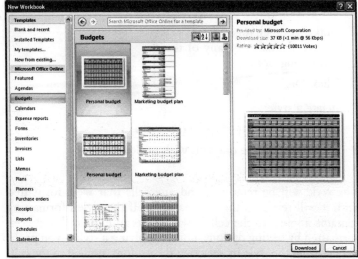

To create a new workbook from any template:

1 Select a **Template Category** from the list on the left of the dialog box.

2 Choose your template – you'll find several online.

3 Click **Create** or **Download**.

You can also create your own templates for workbooks. Using templates can save you time, and also help ensure that workbooks are laid out in a consistent manner.

To create your own template:

1 Create a new workbook (or open an existing workbook).

2 Set it up with the number of sheets and all the standard information, formatting and formulas required, e.g. your company name, logo, column headings, row labels, etc.

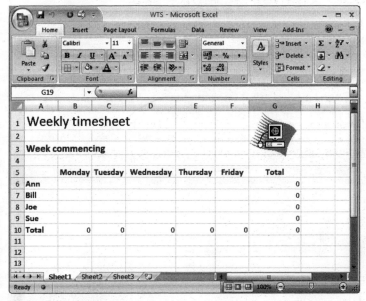

3 Click the Microsoft Office button and then click **Save...**

4 Give your template a name.

5 Select *Excel Template* from the **Save As Type...** list – the **Save in:** field should change to *Templates* automatically.

6 Click **Save**.

7 Close your template file.

♦ Excel workbook and worksheet templates have the .xltx file extension.

To create a new workbook using your template:

1 Click the Microsoft Office button and then **New...**

2 At the **New Workbook** dialog box, double-click **My Templates...** in the **Featuring** category.

3 Select your template from the **My Templates** tab in the **New** dialog box.

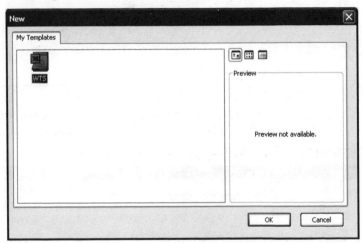

4 Click **OK**.

♦ You will have a new workbook, that contains all the standard information that you put in your template.

5 Complete your workbook and save it in the normal way (not as a template).

♦ You can reuse your Template any time you need to create a new workbook following its layout.

To update your template:

1 Create a workbook using your template.

2 Edit your workbook as required.

3 Save the file as a template, using the same filename as the original.

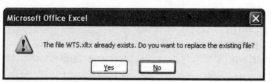

4 At the prompt, click **Yes** to override the existing template.

5 Close your file.

8.3 Worksheet templates

You can also create templates for the worksheets that you add to your workbooks. Previews can make them easier to identify.

To create a custom worksheet template:

1 Create a workbook consisting of one sheet only.

2 Add any standard text, formatting, formulas, headers and footers, etc. to the worksheet.

To add a preview for display in the Insert dialog box:

1 Click the Microsoft Office button.

2 Choose **Finish**, then **Properties**.

3 The **Properties Panel** will be displayed under the Ribbon.

4 Update the Standard properties as required.

To switch on the Preview option:

1 Click **Standard,** and choose **Advanced...** from the list.

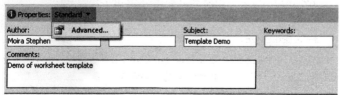

- Notice that the entries you made on the Standard panel are displayed in the dialog box.

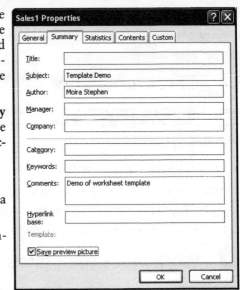

2 On the **Summary** tab, select the **Save preview picture**.

3 Click **OK**.

4 Save your file as a template.

5 Close the template.

- Close the **Properties** panel – click the **Close** button on its title bar.

To insert a worksheet template:

1 Right-click on a sheet tab within your workbook and click **Insert...** on the pop-up menu.

2 Select the template on the **General** tab in the **Insert** dialog box.

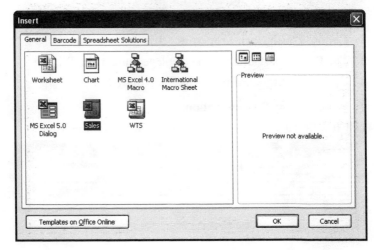

3 Click **OK**.

The new sheet will be inserted to the left of the selected one.

8.4 Chart templates

If you have set up a customized chart layout that you wish to reuse for other charts, you can save it as a chart template (.crtx extension).

To save a chart layout as a template:

1 Select the chart you wish to make into a template.

2 In the **Type** group on the **Design** tab, click **Save Template**.

3 Ensure that the *Charts* folder (within the *Templates* folder) is selected.

4 Give your chart template a name.

5 Click **Save**.

To apply your template when creating a new chart:

1 In the **Charts** group on the **Insert** tab, click any chart button and choose **All Chart Types...,** or click the dialog box launcher at the bottom right of the group.

2 Select **Templates** at the top of the list on the left of the **Create Chart** dialog box.

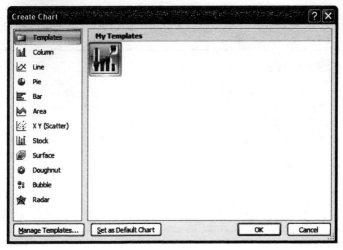

3 Click on the template you want to use and then click **OK**.

To apply a template to an existing chart:

1 Select the chart.

2 Click **Change Chart Type** in the **Type** group on the **Design** tab of the **Chart Tools**.

3 Select **Templates** at the top of the list on the left of the **Create Chart** dialog box.

4 Click on the template you want to use and then click **OK**.

To move or delete a chart template:

1 Display the **Create Chart** dialog box.

2 Click **Manage Templates...**

3 **To move the template** – drag it to the folder you want it to be.

4 **To delete the template** – right-click on it, then click **Delete**. Click **Yes** at the prompt.

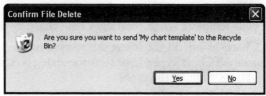

5 Close the **Create Chart** dialog box.

• If you are deleting a chart template, ensure that there are no open workbooks containing charts that are using it.

Summary

We have considered a range of features that enable you to automate and customize many of your data and chart formatting routines in this chapter. We have discussed:

• Creating and managing your own styles

• Workbook templates

• Worksheet templates

• Chart templates.

09

managing lists and tables

In this chapter you will learn:

- how to sort data
- about filtering data
- how to validate data
- how to insert subtotals
- how to manipulate data using Database functions

9.1 Terminology

Many of your worksheets will contain lists of data – stock items, customer contact details, exam results, etc. Excel has facilities to sort, find, filter and extract data from these lists. The tasks that you might want to perform on them are often similar to those you would expect to carry out on a database table in Access. Because of the similarity between the working with your data in this way in Excel and in a database, the terminology used is that usually associated with databases.

- Each row is a **record**.
- Each column is a **field**.
- The column headings are the **field names**.

9.2 Sort

The data can be sorted into ascending or descending order. You can perform a simple sort, using the entries in one column only, or a more complex sort, sorting on up to 64 columns at a time.

There should be no blank rows or columns inside the area to be sorted. When you sort data, you will normally want the data surrounding the column you are sorting to be included in the sort – so don't select the column, as this will restrict your sort to that column only. Excel will warn you if you do this. The action is not normally recommended as it can move data away from other data that it is associated with. (If you accidentally sort a column on its own, undo the action – [Ctrl]-[Z] – to put things back as they were, and try again.)

Excel assumes that the first row is a header row (with column labels) and doesn't include it in the sort.

To perform a sort on one column:

1 Select any cell in the column you want to sort on.

2 Click the **Sort & Filter** button in the **Editing** group on the **Home** tab.

3 Choose **Sort Smallest to Largest** (for ascending order) or **Sort Largest to Smallest** (for descending order).

To perform a multi-level sort (on up to 64 columns at a time):

1 Select any cell within the area you want to sort.

2 Click the **Sort & Filter** button.

3 Choose **Custom Sort...** to open the **Sort** dialog box.

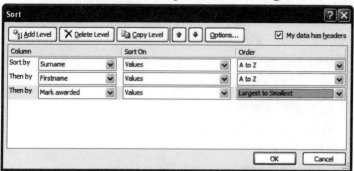

4 Select the main sort column from the **Sort by** list.

5 Set the **Sort On** option – choose *values* if you are sorting by text, number or date or time – or cell colour, font colour or cell icon if you are sorting by format.

6 Choose the **Order**.

7 Click **Add level** to add a column for the second level sort.

8 Repeat steps 4–7 as necessary.

9 Click **OK**.

	A	B	C	D	E
1	\multicolumn{5}{c}{**END OF TERM EXAM RESULTS**}				
2					
3	**Firstname**	**Surname**	**Mark awarded**	**Result**	**Grade**
4	Ann	Allan	48	Fail	Fail
5	Andrew	Borthwick	52	Pass	C
6	Peter	Jackson	91	Pass	A
7	Gill	McLaren	45	Fail	Fail
8	Alison	Smith	50	Pass	C
9	Hector	Smith	68	Pass	B
10	William	Smith	72	Pass	A
11	David	Watson	59	Pass	C
12	Pauline	Watson	65	Pass	B
13	Marion	Williamson	49	Fail	Fail

- Note that Excel assumes your list has a header row – the one that normally contains the column labels or field names. If it doesn't, i.e. you want the first row included in the sort, deselect the **My data has headers** checkbox.

To copy a sort level:

1 Open the Sort dialog box – click the **Sort & Filter** button and then choose **Custom Sort...**

2 Select the sort row you wish to copy.

3 Click **Copy Level** and then **OK**.

To delete a sort level:

1 Open the **Sort** dialog box.

2 Select the sort row you wish to remove.

3 Click **Delete Level** and then **OK**.

To change the sort level of an item:

1 Open the **Sort** dialog box.

2 Select the sort row you wish to move.

3 Click the **Up Arrow** or **Down Arrow** to move the item.

4 Click **OK**.

Sort Options

You can use Sort to rearrange columns of data as well as the rows. The default Sort options are to sort rows of data from top to bottom, and ignore the case (upper or lower) of your text. To make your sort case sensitive, or sort columns from left to right rather than rows from top to bottom, use the Sort Options.

To sort columns:

1 In the row above (or below) the list, type numbers to show the order you want the columns in.

2 Select any cell in the list you want to sort.

3 Open the **Sort** dialog box.

4 Click **Options** in the **Sort** dialog box.

5 Specify the options required.

	A	B	C	D	E
1	**END OF TERM EXAM RESULTS**				
2					
3	2	1	3	5	4
4	**Firstname**	**Surname**	**Mark awarded**	**Result**	**Grade**
5	Ann	Allan	48	Fail	Fail
6	Andrew	Borthwick	52	Pass	C
7	Peter	Jackson	91	Pass	A
8	Gill	McLaren	45	Fail	Fail
9	Alison	Smith	50	Pass	C
10	Hector	Smith	68	Pass	B
11	William	Smith	72	Pass	A
12	David	Watson	59	Pass	C
13	Pauline	Watson	65	Pass	B
14	Marion	Williamson	49	Fail	Fail
15					

6 Click **OK**.

7 Complete the **Sort** dialog box as required – in this example specifying row 3 as the sort row – and click **OK**.

♦ Once your data has been sorted you can delete the row that contains the numbers that specify the sort order.

	A	B	C	D	E
1	**END OF TERM EXAM RESULTS**				
2					
3	1	2	3	4	5
4	**Surname**	**Firstname**	**Mark awarded**	**Grade**	**Result**
5	Allan	Ann	48	Fail	Fail
6	Borthwick	Andrew	52	C	Pass
7	Jackson	Peter	91	A	Pass
8	McLaren	Gill	45	Fail	Fail
9	Smith	Alison	50	C	Pass
10	Smith	Hector	68	B	Pass
11	Smith	William	72	A	Pass
12	Watson	David	59	C	Pass
13	Watson	Pauline	65	B	Pass
14	Williamson	Marion	49	Fail	Fail
15					

9.3 Filtering

Filtering data allows you to quickly extract subsets of your data from a list. When you filter your data, you end up displaying only those records that meet the criteria that you specify. Note that the sort options are also available in the Filter lists.

To filter using 'equal to', to find a match to a specific value:

1 Select any cell in the data range that you want to filter.

2 Click the **Sort & Filter** button in the **Editing** group, and then click **Filter**.

◆ Note that the row containing the headings has filtering enabled on each column.

3 Click the filter arrow in the column you want to use to specify your criteria.

4 Clear the **Select All** checkbox.

5 Tick the checkbox(es) by the criteria you are looking for.

6 Click **OK**.

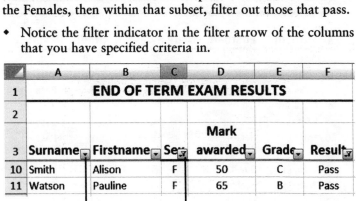

You can filter on more than one column, e.g. to produce a list of all the males or all the females that pass. You could filter out all the Females, then within that subset, filter out those that pass.

◆ Notice the filter indicator in the filter arrow of the columns that you have specified criteria in.

	A	B	C	D	E	F
1	**END OF TERM EXAM RESULTS**					
2						
3	Surname	Firstname	Sex	**Mark** awarded	Grade	Result
10	Smith	Alison	F	50	C	Pass
11	Watson	Pauline	F	65	B	Pass

Filter arrow   Filter indicator

You can filter data using operators other than "equals to" e.g.

> greater than   < less than   <> not equal to

>= greater than or equal to   <= less than or equal to

To use these, select **Number Filters** or **Text Filters**.

1 Click the filter arrow.

2 Select **Number Filters** or **Text Filters** from the options.

3 Select the operator to use or choose **Custom Filter...**

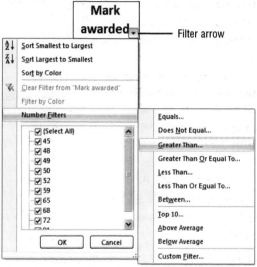

Filter arrow

4 **Above Average** and **Below Average** filter the list immediately. All other options display a dialog box so you can set up your filter criteria.

5 Complete the dialog box – you specify up to two criteria, and use wild card characters (? and *) if you wish.

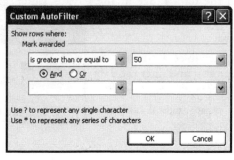

To remove filter criteria:

1 Click the filter arrow in the column you want to remove the filter from.

2 Click **Clear Filter from** *fieldname*.

To remove the filter arrows:

♦ Click the **Sort & Filter** button in the **Editing** group on the **Home** tab, then click **Filter**.

The **Sort and Filter** features are also available on the **Data** tab on the Ribbon.

9.4 Tables

Although you can sort and filter data without creating a table, tables make managing and analysing a set of related data easier. The data within the table is managed independently of data in other columns and rows in the worksheet.

Once created, the main benefits in using a table (compared to working with your data as a basic list) are that you can quickly apply formatting and summary calculation features to the table.

When you convert a data range to a table, the Filter feature is automatically activated.

To create a table:

1 Select the range of data that you wish to identify as a table (or select any cell within the range).

2 Click the **Table** button in the **Table** group on the **Insert** tab (or press [Ctrl]-[T]).

3 Confirm the data range at the **Create Table** dialog box (edit if necessary).

4 Click **OK**.

♦ Filtering is enabled automatically so you can sort and filter the data in your table quickly.

♦ You can create several tables on the one worksheet.

	A	B	C	D	E	F
1	**END OF TERM EXAM RESULTS**					
2						
3	Surname	Firstname	Mark awarded	Grade	Result	
4	Allan	Ann	48	Fail	Fail	
5	Borthwick	Andrew	52	C	Pass	
6	Jackson	Peter	91	A	Pass	
7	McLaren	Gill	45	Fail	Fail	
8	Smith	Alison	50	C	Pass	
9	Smith	Hector	68	B	Pass	
10	Smith	William	72	A	Pass	
11	Watson	David	59	C	Pass	
12	Watson	Pauline	65	B	Pass	
13	Williamson	Marion	49	Fail	Fail	
14						

You can also create a table from the Home tab.

1 Select the range of cells you want to become a table.

2 Click the **Format as Table** button in the Styles group.

3 Select a **Table Style**.

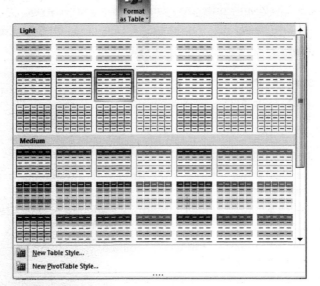

4 Check the cell range and edit if necessary.

5 Click **OK**.

The Table Tools are displayed in the Ribbon.

Sort and filter table data

* You can sort and filter your table data as discussed above.

9.5 Table styles

Tables can be formatted quickly and effectively using the styles.

To apply or change a table style:

1 Select any cell in your table.

2 Display the **Table Style** options on the **Table Tools Design** tab, or the **Home** tab.

3 Click on the style you want to use.

To enable/disable different elements of the table style:

Select or deselect the options in the Table Style Options group:

* **Header Row** – sets the first row as field names with the filter feature enabled.

* **Last Column** – applies formatting to the last column.

* **Totals Row** – adds a totals row, where you can perform summary calculations.

* **Banded Rows** – formats the rows with alternating shading (fill) effects.

* **First Column** – applies formatting to the first column in the table.

* **Banded Columns** – formats the columns with alternating shading (fill) effects.

This next table has Header Row (displayed automatically when you create a table), Totals Row, First Row and Last Column and Banded Rows options selected.

	A	B	C	D	E	F
1			END OF TERM EXAM RESULTS			
2						
3	Surname	Firstname	Sex	Mark awarded	Grade	Result
4	Allan	Ann	F	48	Fail	Fail
5	Borthwick	Andrew	M	52	C	Pass
6	Jackson	Peter	M	91	A	Pass
7	McLaren	Gill			Fail	Fail
8	Smith	William		None	A	Pass
9	Smith	Hector		Average	B	Pass
10	Smith	Alison		Count	C	Pass
11	Watson	Pauline		Count Numbers	B	Pass
12	Watson	David		Max	C	Pass
				Min		
				Sum		
				StdDev		
13	Williamson	Marion		Var	Fail	Fail
				More Functions...		
14	Total			59.9		10

When the Header Row option is selected, the labels in the header row remain visible when you scroll through a long table. They replace the worksheet headers (A, B, C...) so that you always know what the information in your columns is.

	Surname	Firstname	Sex	Mark awarded	Grade	Result
10	Smith	Alison	F	50	C	Pass
11	Watson	Pauline	F	65	B	Pass
12	Watson	David	M	59	C	Pass
13	Williamson	Marion	F	49	Fail	Fail
14	Total			59.9		10

The functions in the *Total* row are **Average** for the *Mark Awarded* and **Count** for the *Result*. You can change the function used in any cell by clicking the arrow within the cell and selecting the function required from the list.

The other Table Style options are formatting options.

To create your own table style:

1 Display the **Table** styles.

2 Click **New Table Style...**

3 Select the table element to specify the formatting for.

4 Click **Format**.

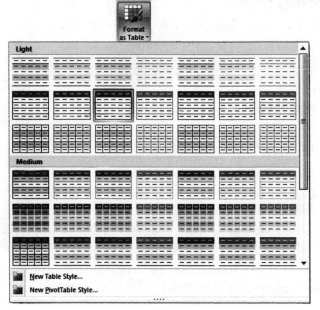

5 Set up the font, fill and border formats required.

6 Click **OK**.

7 Repeat steps 3–6 for each element.

8 Click **OK** at the **New Table Quick Style** dialog box.

◆ Your style will be displayed at the top of the Table Styles list, in the Custom category.

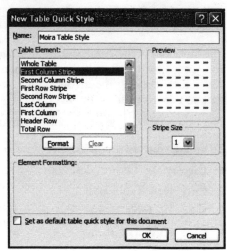

Printing a table

If the data is in a table, you can print just the Excel table.

1 Select any cell within the table to activate it.

2 Click the Microsoft Office button, then click **Print**.

3 In **Print what:** select *Table*.

4 Click **OK**.

Restore table to data range

To remove the table attribute from a range of data:

1 Click anywhere in the table to activate the Table tools.

2 In the **Tools** group, click **Convert to Range**, then click **Yes** at the prompt.

9.6   Advanced Filter

If you want to keep a set of filter criteria for future use, you must use the Advanced Filter option. This requires you to specify the criteria you wish to apply on a separate area of the worksheet (usually above it). The criteria in this range are then applied to your list of data.

The process has two steps:

• Set up the criteria range.

• Apply the criteria in the range to your list of data.

To set up the criteria range:

1 Copy the column headings (field names) to a blank area in your worksheet, above the rows you are filtering (insert some blank rows if necessary)

2 Specify the criteria in the rows under the copied headings:

• If you enter several conditions in one row, Excel will only return a record where all the conditions in the row are met.

• If you enter several conditions in different rows, Excel will return the records that meet any of the conditions specified on any individual row.

The screenshot below gives examples of valid criteria.

	A	B	C	D	E	F	G
2							
3	Surname	Firstname	Sex	Mark awarded		Grade	Result
4	Smith		M	>70			
5							
6	Surname	Firstname	Sex	Mark awarded		Grade	Result
7	<t						<>Fail
8							
9	Surname	Firstname	Sex	Mark awarded	Mark awarded	Grade	Result
10				>=60	<=80		
11							
12	Surname	Firstname	Sex	Mark awarded		Grade	Result
13	Allan						
14	Smith						
15							

- The first example will list all Smiths, who are Male and had a mark of over 70.

- The second will return all with surnames before T in the alphabet, and who also did not fail.

- The third will display all who were awarded a mark between 60 and 80 (inclusive).

- The fourth will list those with the surname Allan or Smith.

To apply the conditions set in the criteria range:

1 Select any cell in the list of data that you want to extract records from.

2 On the **Data** tab, click **Advanced** in the **Sort & Filter** group.

3 At the **Advanced Filter** dialog box, select the **Action** – *Filter the list, in-place* or *Copy to another location*.

4 Check and edit, if necessary, the **List range:** – the cells with the data.

5 Set the **Criteria range:** – the cells containing your criteria. You must include the field name row as well as all the rows containing the criteria.

6 If you selected **Copy to another location**, set the location for the extracted records. You only need to specify the top leftmost cell of where the results are to appear.

7 Click **OK**.

• If you filtered the list in place, click [⚡ Clear] in the **Sort & Filter** group to display all your records again.

Select columns

When you filter in place, all columns are displayed in the result. If you filter to another location, you can specify which columns to include in the copy operation.

To specify the columns:

1 Copy the labels for the required columns to the first row of the area where you plan to paste the filtered rows.

2 When you filter, enter a reference to the cells containing the copied column labels in the **Copy to** box.

The copied rows will then include only the columns for which you copied the labels.

9.7 Data validation

When entering data into a worksheet, you will want to try to ensure, as far as is practicable, that the data is accurate. To help achieve this, you can set up validation rules for any cell or range of cells where you want to check the validity of the data entered.

By default, each cell in a worksheet will accept any value. However, you can limit the range of acceptable entries by setting up validation rules. In our Student Results worksheet, we could set a rule for the data area in the Mark awarded column so that it would only accept values between 0 and 100. Anything over 100 or less than 0 would not be accepted and an error message would be displayed.

To set a validation rule:

1 Select the cell(s) that you want the rule to apply to (do not include the column heading or any other cells).

2 Click **Data Validation** in the
   Data Tools group on the **Data**
   tab.

3 On the **Settings** tab, complete the validation criteria fields.

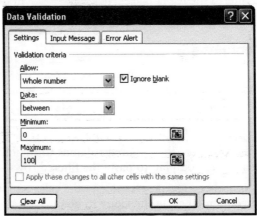

4 If you want a message displayed when the cell is selected,
   enter it on the **Input Message** tab.

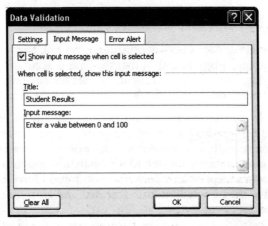

5 If you want a specific message to appear when the rule is not
   met, enter it on the **Error Alert** tab (a default message appears if you don't set up your own).

6 Click **OK**.

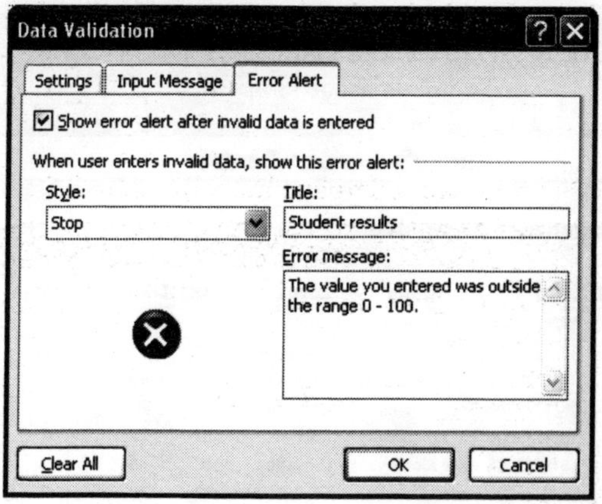

En la imagen se ve un cuadro de diálogo de Data Validation.

- When you select a cell with a validation rule, the **Input Message** will be displayed.

  Student Results
  Enter a value
  between 0 and 100

- If you enter invalid data into a cell, the **Error Alert** message will be displayed.

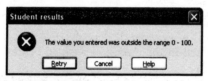

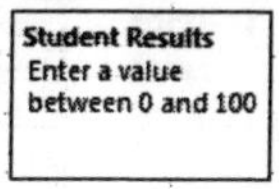

To remove a validation rule from your cells:

1 Select the cell(s) you want to remove the rule from.

2 Click **Data Validation** in the **Data Tools** group.

3 Click **Clear All** and then **OK**.

9.8 Subtotals

Lists of data can be summarized automatically using subtotals. In this example, customers buy stems of flowers from a garden centre. The centre wants to know the total value of orders from each customer over the period. The total of each order is calculated using a formula – see the Formula bar in the illustration.

To display subtotals:

1 Sort the data into ascending order on the field that you want to create subtotals after, e.g. *Customer*.

185

managing lists and tables 09

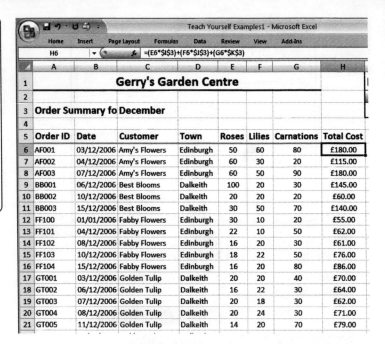

	Teach Yourself Examples1 - Microsoft Excel
Home	Insert Page Layout Formulas Data Review View Add-Ins

H6   =(E6*$I$3)+(F6*$J$3)+(G6*$K$3)

	A	B	C	D	E	F	G	H
1			Gerry's Garden Centre					
2								
3	Order Summary fo December							
4								
5	Order ID	Date	Customer	Town	Roses	Lilies	Carnations	Total Cost
6	AF001	03/12/2006	Amy's Flowers	Edinburgh	50	60	80	£180.00
7	AF002	04/12/2006	Amy's Flowers	Edinburgh	60	30	20	£115.00
8	AF003	07/12/2006	Amy's Flowers	Edinburgh	60	50	90	£180.00
9	BB001	06/12/2006	Best Blooms	Dalkeith	100	20	30	£145.00
10	BB002	10/12/2006	Best Blooms	Dalkeith	20	20	20	£60.00
11	BB003	15/12/2006	Best Blooms	Dalkeith	30	50	70	£140.00
12	FF100	01/01/2006	Fabby Flowers	Edinburgh	30	10	20	£55.00
13	FF101	04/12/2006	Fabby Flowers	Edinburgh	22	10	50	£62.00
14	FF102	08/12/2006	Fabby Flowers	Edinburgh	16	20	30	£61.00
15	FF103	10/12/2006	Fabby Flowers	Edinburgh	18	22	50	£76.00
16	FF104	15/12/2006	Fabby Flowers	Edinburgh	16	20	80	£86.00
17	GT001	03/12/2006	Golden Tulip	Dalkeith	20	20	40	£70.00
18	GT002	06/12/2006	Golden Tulip	Dalkeith	16	22	30	£64.00
19	GT003	07/12/2006	Golden Tulip	Dalkeith	20	18	30	£62.00
20	GT004	08/12/2006	Golden Tulip	Dalkeith	20	24	30	£71.00
21	GT005	11/12/2006	Golden Tulip	Dalkeith	14	20	70	£79.00

2 Select any cell in the data you wish to create subtotals for.

3 Click **Subtotal** in the **Outline** group on the **Data** tab to display the **Subtotal** dialog box.

4 In the **At each change in:** field, select the item you wish to subtotal on – *Customer* in this example.

5 Select the function from the **Use function:** list (*Sum* if you want subtotals).

6 In the **Add subtotal to:** list, tick a box to indicate where to display the subtotal.

7 Select/deselect the checkboxes as required.

8 Click **OK**.

The result is a list showing the data grouped and subtotalled.

| H9 | ▾ | fx | =SUBTOTAL(9,H6:H8) |
| | | | |

1 2 3		B	C	D	E	F	G	H	Pr
	1		**Gerry's Garden Centre**						
	2								
	3	mmary fo	December						
	4								
	5	Date	Customer	Town	Roses	Lilies	Carnations	Total Cost	
+	9		Amy's Flowers Total					£475.00	
+	13		Best Blooms Total					£345.00	
+	19		Fabby Flowers Total					£340.00	
+	27		Golden Tulip Total					£504.00	
−	28		Grand Total					£1,664.00	

The outline pane on the left can be used to expand and collapse the level of detail. In the example here, Level 1 = Grand Total, Level 2 = Item Subtotal, Level 3 = Detail. You can display the amount of detail required by clicking the level numbers at the top of the pane.

* You can collapse and expand groups within the list by clicking the Hide ▬ and Show ✚ buttons in the outline pane.

* To clear the outline, click the **Subtotal** button, then click **Remove All** in the **Subtotal** dialog box.

Subtotal functions

There are 11 subtotal functions, with a different code depending on whether you want to include hidden values in your result:

Function_num (includes hidden values)	Function_num (ignores hidden values)	Function
1	101	AVERAGE
2	102	COUNT
3	103	COUNTA
4	104	MAX
5	105	MIN
6	106	PRODUCT
7	107	STDEV
8	108	STDEVP
9	109	SUM
10	110	VAR
11	111	VARP

It is normally easiest to enter subtotals using the above procedure. The subtotal function is entered automatically to calculate the subtotal for each group and also for the complete range (giving the grand total). Once a subtotal function is entered you can easily edit it directly in the Formula bar if you wish.

To edit the subtotal function:

1 Select the cell that contains the function.

2 Remove the function number from the function in the Formula bar.

3 Right-click, and choose **Pick From Drop-down List**.

4 Double-click on the function to use in your **Subtotal**.

5 Press [**Enter**].

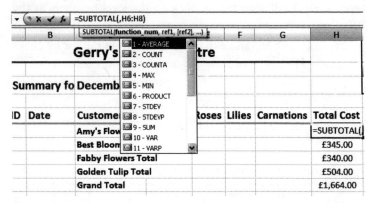

9.9 Database functions

DCOUNT

DCOUNT looks at a list of values, finds the rows that satisfy specific criteria, and counts them. It's used when you want to count the values that match more than one criterion.

Set up a criteria range – see section 9.6, Advanced Filter.

To insert the DCOUNT function:

1 Select the cell that you want the answer to appear in.

2 Click the **Insert Function** dialog box launcher (bottom right of the **Function Library** group on the **Formulas** tab).

3 Select the **Database** category and then **DCOUNT** from the Function list.

4 Click **OK**. The **Function Arguments** dialog box will open. This is where you will specify the details of the function.

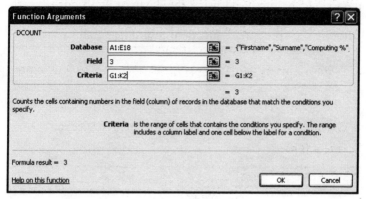

5 Enter the range of cells that your list of data fills in the **Database** field.

6 For the **Field,** enter the column label or number that you want to base the count on (it must be a numeric column).

7 Specify the range that the **Criteria** are in.

8 Click **OK**.

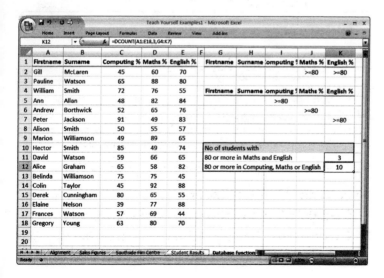

DSUM, DMIN, DMAX

Other functions that work along the same principle are DSUM, DMIN and DMAX. In the example below, Excel is used to keep details of orders for cut flowers from retail outlets. Summary data could be produced using the database functions. Experiment with these (following the steps as for DCOUNT, but substituting the appropriate function) to produce summary data.

	Teach Yourself Examples1 - Microsoft Excel
Home Insert Page Layout Formulas Data Review View Add-Ins	
K15	fx =DSUM(A5:F23,"Roses",H5:K6)

	A	B	C	D	E	F	G	H	I	J	K
1			Gerry's Garden Centre								
2											
3	Order Summary for		December								
4											
5	Order ID	Date	Customer	Roses	Lilies	Carnations		Customer			
6	FF100	01/01/2006	Fabby Flowers	30	10	20		Fabby Flowers			
7	GT001	03/12/2006	Golden Tulip	20	20	40					
8	AF001	03/12/2006	Amy's Flowers	50	60	80		Customer			
9	FF101	04/12/2006	Fabby Flowers	22	10	50		Golden Tulip			
10	AF002	04/12/2006	Amy's Flowers	60	30	20					
11	GT002	06/12/2006	Golden Tulip	16	22	30		No of orders from Fabby Flowers			5
12	BB001	06/12/2006	Best Blooms	100	20	30		Roses			
13	GT003	07/12/2006	Golden Tulip	20	18	30		Minimum no ordered by Fabby Flowers			16
14	AF003	07/12/2006	Amy's Flowers	60	50	90		Maximum no ordered by Fabby Flowers			30
15	FF102	08/12/2006	Fabby Flowers	16	20	30		Total no ordered by Fabby Flowers			102
16	GT004	08/12/2006	Golden Tulip	20	24	30					
17	FF103	10/12/2006	Fabby Flowers	18	22	50		No of orders from Golden Tulip			7
18	BB002	10/12/2006	Best Blooms	20	20	20		Roses			
19	GT005	11/12/2006	Golden Tulip	14	20	70		Minimum no ordered by Golden Tulip			14
20	GT006	12/12/2006	Golden Tulip	14	16	60		Maximum no ordered by Golden Tulip			20
21	FF104	15/12/2006	Fabby Flowers	16	20	80		Total no ordered by Golden Tulip			124
22	BB003	15/12/2006	Best Blooms	30	50	70					
23	GT006	16/12/2006	Golden Tulip	20	30	50					
24											

Summary

In this chapter we have discussed:

♦ Database terminology

♦ Sorting data ranges on a single field and multi-level sorts

♦ Using sort to rearrange columns

♦ Filtering data

♦ Excel tables

♦ Advanced Filter

♦ Validation rules

♦ Subtotals

♦ Database functions.

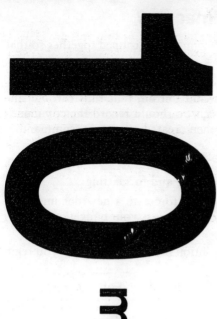

10

macros

In this chapter you will learn:

- what macros are
- how to record, run, edit and delete macros
- about making your macros available to all workbooks

10.1 What are macros?

A macro is a set of Excel commands grouped together so that you can execute them as a single command.

If you perform a task often, but cannot find an Excel keyboard shortcut, or command button, that runs through the sequence you want to use, you should record the commands into a macro. You have then created a 'custom' command.

What could you use a macro for?

- Speeding up routine editing and formatting.
- Recording the instructions to create a new document using one of your own templates, e.g. your budget or monthly sales figures.
- Quickly accessing an option in a dialog box that you regularly use.
- Combining a group of commands you often execute in the same sequence.

There are two ways to create macros in Excel:

- **Recording** – we will be using this option. You can record any function that you can access through the menus and dialog boxes.
- **Visual Basic Editor** – you can record powerful, flexible macros using this. These macros can include Visual Basic as well as Excel commands. We will take a brief excursion into the Editor when we discuss editing macros.

The basic Macro commands (to record, stop recording and play) are displayed at the left end of the status bar. You will also find them on the Developer tab. If it ‎‏Ready‏‎ is not visible, to display it:

1 Click the Microsoft Office button and choose **Excel Options**.

2 In the **Popular** area, select **Show Developer tab in the Ribbon**.

3 Click **OK**.

The Developer tab

10.2 Recording your macro

Before you start recording your macro, think through what it is that you want to record. If there are any commands that you're not sure about, try them out first to check that they do what you want to record. Try recording a simple macro that creates a new workbook using one of your own templates.

To create your new workbook, you must:

1 Click the Microsoft Office button and choose **New...**

2 Click **My Templates...** in the **Templates** panel.

3 Select the template.

4 Click **OK**.

The next example uses the template set up in Chapter 8.

To record the macro:

1 Click **Record Macro** on the status bar or in the **Code** group of the **Developer** tab.

2 Give your macro a name – something like *MyTemplate* would be appropriate.

♦ Don't use spaces in the macro name – most punctuation characters are also not allowed. If you want to separate words, use the underline character.

3 If you want a keyboard shortcut, click in the **Shortcut** field and enter the shortcut to use, e.g. [**Ctrl**]-[**Shift**]-[**T**].

4 Select the workbook you want to store the macro in.

♦ If you choose the Personal Macro Workbook, your macro will be globally available, in every workbook you create.

5 Click **OK**.

♦ You will be returned to your worksheet, and the Macro buttons on the status bar and the Ribbon have changed to **Stop Recording**.

6 Work through the steps you want to record.

7 Click the **Stop** button when you've finished. Recording has saved the macro automatically.

Make your macros available

If you record a macro in your Personal Macro Workbook, you can access it from anywhere using the keyboard shortcut, or run the macro from the Macro dialog box.

10.3 Playing back your macro

You can play back a macro using the keyboard shortcut (if you specified one) or by using the Play Macro buttons.

To use the keyboard shortcut:

• Press the keyboard shortcut you recorded, e.g. [Ctrl]-[Shift]-[T] to create your new workbook.

To use the command buttons:

1 Click the **Play Macro/Run Macro** button on the status bar or the **Code** group of the **Developer** tab.

2 At the **Macro** dialog box, select your macro from the list.

3 Click **Run**.

The given example is a simple one to illustrate how a macro can be recorded and executed. You will find that macros are especially useful when you have long sequences of commands to work through.

10.4 Ideas for more macros

You can record almost anything you want into a macro. Some of the things that you could record into a macro may also be automated in other ways, e.g. Styles. Macros are usually used to carry out a sequence of commands.

If you find that you regularly use a series of commands in the same order, or use an option that is buried deep in a dialog box, macros can help you speed up the way you work.

Try out the following macros to get some more practice. They are all easy to set up.

Setting up a Header and/or Footer

If you use the same header and/or footer in many of your workbooks, you could record the sequence of commands into a macro.

♦ DO NOT use the **Header and Footer** button in the Text group on the **Insert** tab for this – use the **Page Layout** dialog box.

1 Click **Record Macro** on the status bar or in the **Code** group of the **Developer** tab.

2 Give your macro a name – *HeaderFooter* or similar.

3 Set a keyboard shortcut if you wish e.g. [Ctrl]-[Shift]-[F].

4 Select the workbook you want to store the macro in.

5 Click **OK**.

♦ Now it's time to add a header and/or footer to your pages.

6 Go to the **Page Layout** tab.

7 Launch the **Page Layout** dialog box – click the launcher at the bottom right of any group on the **Page Layout** tab.

8 Select the **Header and Footer** tab in the **Page Setup** dialog box.

9 Use the **Custom Header** and **Custom Footer** options to set up your header and footer as required.

10 Click **OK** to close the dialog box.

11 Stop recording.

Discount calculator

Let's say you offer a discount to your customers based on the amount of their order. You could record a discount calculator into a macro in your Personal Macro Workbook, then access the calculator from any workbook. This macro will:

◆ Create a new blank worksheet within your workbook.

◆ Enter the text and formula to the discount calculator.

◆ Protect the sheet so that only the *Amount of Order* details can be entered.

1 Create a new workbook, or open an existing one.

2 Start to record a new macro. Call it *DiscountCal* or something similar.

3 Set up a keyboard shortcut if you want one.

4 Select the workbook to store the macro in.

5 Click **OK**.

6 Insert a new worksheet.

7 Enter the text and the formula to calculate the discount (in this example 7.5%) and balance due (see below – don't display the formulas).

D16		
	A	B
1	Total Amount of Order	
2		
3	Discount	=B1*7.5%
4		
5	Balance Due	=B1-B3
6		

8 Format the cells to **Currency**.

9 Unlock the cell that will take the *Amount of order* and protect the worksheet (see section 5.10).

10 Stop recording.

10.5 Deleting a macro

As you experiment with setting up macros, you will inevitably end up with some that you don't want to keep. They may not prove as useful as you first thought, or they might not run properly. You can delete any macro you no longer require.

If the macro you want to delete is in the Personal Macro Workbook, you must 'unhide' the workbook before you can delete it.

To unhide a workbook:

1 Click the **Unhide** button in the **Window** group on the **View** tab.

2 Select the workbook – *Personal* in this case.

3 Click **OK**.

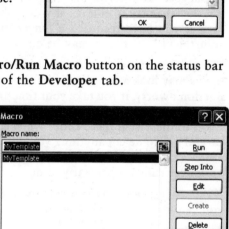

To delete a macro:

1 Click the **Play Macro/Run Macro** button on the status bar or the **Code** group of the **Developer** tab.

2 Choose **Macros...**

3 Select the macro you want to delete from the list.

4 Click **Delete**.

5 Confirm the deletion at the prompt.

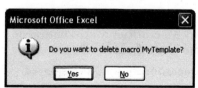

If you have displayed your Personal Macro Workbook, you must hide it again once you've deleted any macros you don't want to keep. Do not close it – if you do you won't be able to use the macros that you recorded in the workbook.

To hide the Personal Macro Workbook again:

♦ Click **Hide** in the **Window** group on the **View** tab.

10.6 Editing a macro

I'd suggest you re-record any short macro that has an error in it rather than try to edit it – it will probably be quicker. However, if you have recorded a longer macro or have a minor adjustment to make, it may be quicker to edit it.

The macros you record are translated into Visual Basic – so things may look a bit strange when you first try editing them. But don't worry, if you take your time and have a look through the instructions you'll soon be able to relate your actions in Excel to the Visual Basic code. When editing a macro, be very careful not to delete anything you don't understand, or insert anything that should not be there – you might find your macro no longer runs properly if you do.

If the worst comes to the worst and the macro stops working, you can always record it again.

The Visual Basic code will often have far more lines of code than the number of commands you intentionally recorded. Don't worry about this – some instructions are picked up from default settings in dialog boxes. Just scroll through until you see something you recognize as the line you want to change.

Let's try editing the discount amount in our discount calculator to make it 12.5%. If the discount calculator macro is in the Personal Macro Workbook, you must unhide the workbook before you can edit it.

To edit the macro:

1 Click the **Play Macro/Run Macro** button on either the status bar or the **Code** group of the **Developer** tab.

2 Select your macro from the list displayed.

3 Click **Edit**.

- The Visual Basic code for the macro will be displayed
4 Scroll through the code to find the area you want to change.

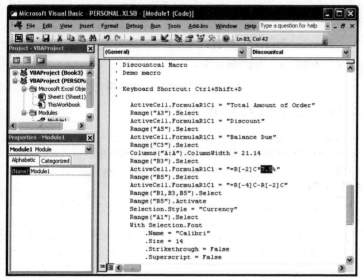

5 Edit as required.
6 Save the changes – click the **Save** tool on the Visual Basic Standard toolbar.
7 Close the Visual Basic window – click the **Close** button at the right of its title bar.

10.7 Saving macros on exit

If you have saved some macros into your Personal Macro Workbook, a prompt will appear when you exit Excel, asking if you want to save the changes to that workbook. If you want to be able to use the macros you have created the next time you use Excel, click **Yes** at the prompt.

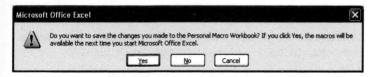

Summary

In this chapter we have given you a brief introduction to Macros. This feature is potentially a very powerful one which cannot be fully developed here. We have introduced you to:

- Recording macros

- Assigning and using keyboard shortcuts

- Running a macro

- Deleting a macro

- Editing a macro using the Visual Basic Editor

- Saving changes to the Personal Macro Workbook.

11

excel with other applications

In this chapter you will learn:

- the difference between linking and embedding
- how to link data in other applications to Excel
- how to use Excel data in a Word Mail Merge

11.1 Get external data

Excel is part of Microsoft Office and integrates very well with the other applications in the suite. If you have the full suite then you have the benefit of being able to use the most appropriate tool for the job, and share your data across the applications.

If you have data held in another application, or a company database, and you want to manipulate it using Excel, you could import it into Excel. This section introduces importing data from external sources.

- See 'File Formats that are supported by Excel' in the Help system for full details.

To get data from Access:

1 Select the cell in the top left corner of the range you want to import into (make sure you have enough empty rows and columns for the data).

2 On the **Data** tab, click **From Access** in the **Get External Data** group.

3 Select your data source and click **Open**.

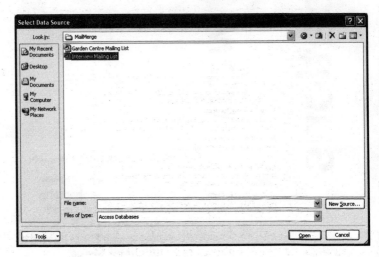

4 Specify how you want to view the imported data, and where you want it placed.

5 Click **OK**.

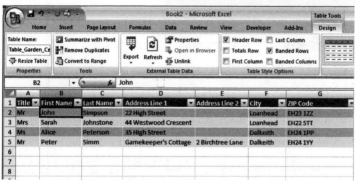

If your Access file contains more than one table, use Microsoft Query to select the table and fields required.

1 Choose **From Microsoft Query** from the **From Other Sources** list, and work through the wizard.

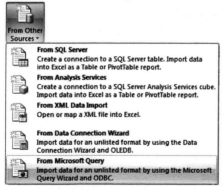

2 At the **Choose Data Source** dialog box, choose **MS Access Database** on the **Databases** tab and click **OK**.

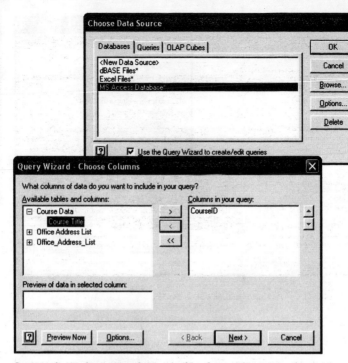

3 At the **Select Database** dialog box, navigate through your folders and select your database and click **OK**.

4 Work through the Query Wizard, selecting your fields, sort order, etc. as you progress through each step.

5 Click **Finish** when you reach the end.

6 Specify how you want to view the imported data, and where you want it placed.

7 Click **OK**.

To get data from the Web:

1 Click **From the Web** in the **Get External Data** group.

2 Locate the web page you want to retrieve data from.

3 Click the arrow next to the table(s) you want to import.

4 Click **Import**.

5 Complete the **Import data** dialog box.

6 Click **OK**.

Import selection arrows

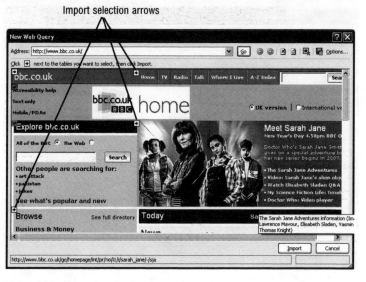

Text files can also be imported easily.

To get data from a text file:

1 Click **From Text** in the **Get External Data** group.

2 At the **Import Text File** dialog box select your file and click **Import**.

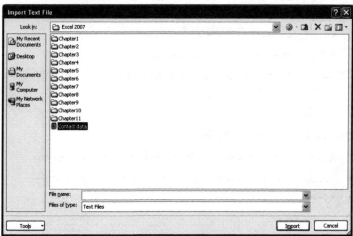

3 Work through the Text Import Wizard.

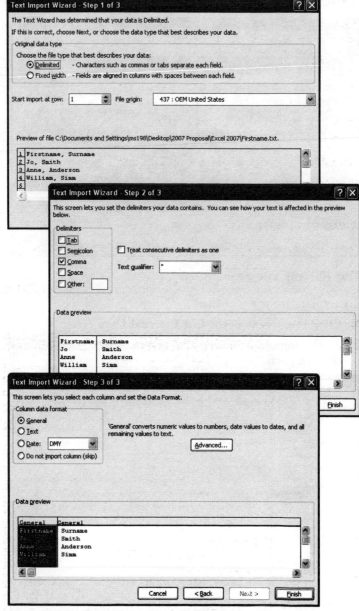

Importing data with the Text Import Wizard – this file used a comma as the delimiter to separate items.

Refresh

Once you have your data imported into Excel, you can easily keep it up to date with the source file.

To refresh your data:

1 Select a cell anywhere within the data range you wish to update.

2 Click the **Refresh** button in the **External Table Data** group.

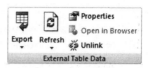

To update more than one set of data at a time:

1 Click the arrow at the bottom of the **Refresh** button.

2 Select **Refresh All**.

Refresh options

1 Click the arrow at the bottom of the **Refresh** button.

2 Select **Connection Properties...**

3 Set the **Refresh** options in the **Connection Properties** dialog box.

4 Click **OK**.

- If you work with imported data, explore the options associated with this topic using the Help system as necessary.

11.2 Linking vs embedding

Linking and embedding are techniques that enable you to exchange data between Excel and other applications. The key differences between linked and embedded data lie in where it is stored and how it is updated.

Linked data

Linked data *is not* stored in your Excel workbook. It is stored in a file, e.g. a document or presentation, in the source application (the one in which it was created). The data is updated within the source application – and those changes are reflected in the Excel workbook to which it is linked.

Advantages of linking data include:

- The Excel workbook is smaller than with embedded data.
- The data in the Excel workbook reflects the current status of the source data.

Embedded data

Embedded data *is* stored in your Excel workbook. If the source data changes, those changes will not be reflected in the workbook. However, when you create and edit the data, you have access to all the functions within the source application.

Advantages of embedding data:

- All the data is held in one file.
- You have access to powerful functions that are not part of the Excel application when creating and editing the object.

The following sections discuss some of the methods you can use to integrate the data across the applications in Office 2007.

11.3   Copy and Paste

You can copy text, data, graphics, charts, etc. from one application to another within the Office suite using simple copy and paste techniques. We will consider how you can copy charts and data *from* Excel into other applications in the Office suite.

To copy and paste:

1   Start Excel *and* the application you want to copy the data or chart to.

2   Open the workbook that you are copying from, and the file that will receive the copy.

3   Select the chart or data you want to copy.

4   Click the **Copy** button in the **Clipboard** group on the **Home** tab.

5   Switch to the application you want to copy the data or chart into.

6   Place the insertion point where you want the data or chart to appear.

7   Click the **Paste** button in the **Clipboard** group.

When you copy charts and data in this way, the chart or data is not 'linked' to the original data in the Excel workbook in any way. Should you edit the data in Excel, the data you copied into the destination file remains as it was when you copied it.

You can copy and paste data from Excel into a Word document, a PowerPoint presentation or an Access database. When you copy and paste data into these applications the data is displayed in a table in the destination application.

You can also copy and paste charts from Excel into a Word document or a PowerPoint presentation.

11.4   Linking data

If you want the data that you copy into your file to be kept in line with the data held in Excel, you should create a link to it. You can use the Paste options or Copy and Paste Special to create a link.

To link data:

1 Start Excel *and* the application you want to copy data to.

2 Select the chart or data you want to copy.

3 Click the **Copy** button in the **Clipboard** group.

4 Switch to the application you want to copy into.

5 Place the insertion point where you want the chart or data to appear.

6 Paste the data using the **Paste** button.

7 Click the **Paste options** button.

8 Choose a link option.

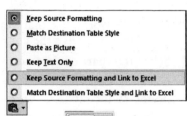

Or

9 Click the arrow under the **Paste** button and choose **Paste Special...**

10 Select the **Paste Link** button.

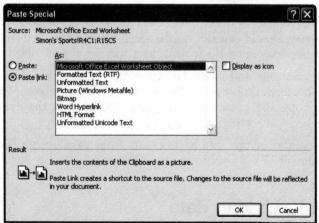

11 Choose an option from the **As:** list – when you select one a brief description of its effect appears in the **Result** box.

12 Click **OK**.

When copied in this way, the chart or data displayed in the destination file is linked to the original data in Excel. Should you edit the data in Excel, it will be updated automatically in your Word document or PowerPoint presentation.

11.5 Embedding data

You can copy and paste, or use Paste Special to get data or charts from Excel into a file in Word or PowerPoint. However, if you want data in Word or PowerPoint, and it isn't already set up in Excel (and doesn't need to be), you can insert a worksheet into a Word or PowerPoint file. It will be created and edited using Excel functions.

The Excel Worksheet you insert will be an embedded object.

To insert a Microsoft Excel Worksheet:

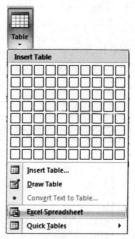

1 Place the insertion point where you want the worksheet to appear in your Word document or PowerPoint presentation.

2 Click the arrow under the **Table** button on the **Insert** tab.

3 In Word choose **Excel Spreadsheet**.

♦ In PowerPoint choose **Insert Excel Table...**

4 An embedded worksheet is inserted, with the Excel Ribbon displayed.

5 Set up your worksheet as normal.

6 Click anywhere outside the worksheet area when you've finished to return to your Word or PowerPoint file.

◆ To edit your worksheet, double-click on it to activate it and the Excel commands.

11.6 Mail Merge

Data in an Excel workbook can be used as the data document in a Mail Merge in Word. From the worksheets that have been set up in this book, the student results worksheet could be merged into a Word document so that we could send letters out to our students telling them how well they had done in their exams. You could add columns to contain the student address details to the worksheet.

1 The top row of your data should contain the field names. Enter the data that will be merged into your document on the worksheet starting under the field name row.

	A	B	C	D	E	F	G	H
1	**Firstname**	**Surname**	**Mark awarded**	**Result**	**Grade**	**Address**	**Town**	
2	Gill	McLaren	45	Fail	Fail	10 Gamekeepers Way	Aberdeen	
3	Alison	Smith	50	Pass	C	75 Scott Street	Aberdeen	
4	Ann	Allan	48	Fail	Fail	14 Brunsfield Terrace	Dalkeith	
5	David	Watson	59	Pass	C	15 St Stephen Street	Dalkeith	
6	Andrew	Borthwick	52	Pass	C	25 Potters Row	Edinburgh	
7	Hector	Smith	68	Pass	B	33 Andrew's Walk	Edinburgh	
8	Peter	Jackson	91	Pass	A	61 Milton Park	Glasgow	
9	William	Smith	72	Pass	A	100b St John's Road	Livingston	
10	Pauline	Watson	65	Pass	B	15 High Street	Stirling	
11	Marion	Williamson	49	Fail	Fail	10 Gillespie Cescent	Stirling	
12								

2 In Word, set up your Mail Merge document in the normal way. Select your Excel workbook when you open your DataSource.

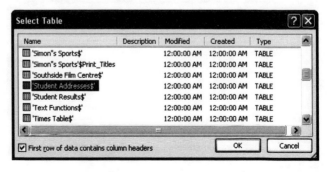

Select Table					? ✕
Name	Description	Modified	Created	Type	
▦ 'Simon"s Sports$'		12:00:00 AM	12:00:00 AM	TABLE	
▦ 'Simon"s Sports'$Print_Titles		12:00:00 AM	12:00:00 AM	TABLE	
▦ 'Southside Film Centre$'		12:00:00 AM	12:00:00 AM	TABLE	
▦ 'Student Addresses$'		12:00:00 AM	12:00:00 AM	TABLE	
▦ 'Student Results$'		12:00:00 AM	12:00:00 AM	TABLE	
▦ 'Text Functions$'		12:00:00 AM	12:00:00 AM	TABLE	
▦ 'Times Table$'		12:00:00 AM	12:00:00 AM	TABLE	

☑ First row of data contains column headers   [OK] [Cancel]

3 Choose the sheet required, or select the named range that contains the data you wish to use.

4 Complete the Main Document in Word using the fields from your worksheet.

Summary

In this chapter we have discussed some of the ways you can integrate Excel with the rest of the Microsoft Office suite. We have considered:

- Importing data from Access, the Web and text files
- The difference between linking and embedding data
- Copy and Paste
- Linking the source data in an Excel workbook with the copy in Word or PowerPoint using Copy and Paste Special
- Embedding a worksheet in Word and in PowerPoint
- Merging an Excel list into a Word Mail Merge document.

12

excel and the web

In this chapter you will learn:

- how to send your workbooks by e-mail and fax
- about hyperlinks
- how to set up your data on web pages

12.1 E-mail and fax

Provided you have a modem, communications software and a service provider, you can e-mail your Excel workbook to anywhere in the world. E-mail is usually very fast – sometimes your message will be delivered almost instantly, other times it may take an hour or so.

You can e-mail an open workbook directly from Excel. The whole workbook can be sent as a file attachment to the message or the current worksheet can be sent, as text, as the body of the message – though this option is only available if Outlook or Outlook Express is your default e-mail application.

To e-mail a workbook from within Excel:

1 Open the workbook you want to e-mail.
2 Click the Microsoft Office button.
3 Select **Send**, and then **E-mail** to send the workbook as an attachment.

Or

◆ Select **Send**, then **Internet Fax** to fax your workbook (you must be signed up with a Fax Service to use this option).

4 Complete the mail message/fax message and send.

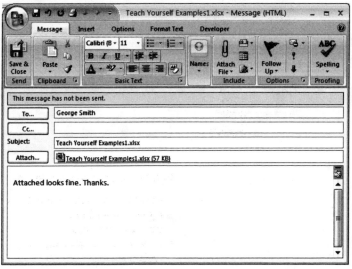

To attach a workbook from within your mail software:

1 Click the **Create a New Mail Message** tool.

2 Enter the addresses in the **To:** field and **Cc:** field if necessary.

3 Type in your subject.

4 Key in your message.

5 Click the **Attach** tool.

6 In the **Open file** dialog box, select the file and click **Attach**.

7 Repeat steps 5–6 if you want more than one file attached.

8 Send your message.

12.2 Hyperlinks

A hyperlink is a 'hot spot' that lets you jump from your workbook to another location – on your own computer, on your company network or anywhere in the world via the Internet.

Adding hyperlinks

You can insert a hyperlink anywhere in your workbook. When you click one, the file that it points to is displayed on screen.

To insert a hyperlink to a file on your system:

1 Select the cell you want to place the hyperlink in.

2 Click the **Hyperlink** button in the **Links** group on

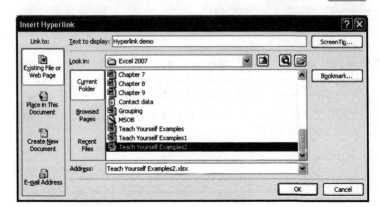

the **Insert** tab.

3 Select *Existing File or Web page* in the **Link to:** options.

4 Enter your display text – this is what will appear in your workbook.

5 Locate and select the file you want to link to.

6 Click **OK**.

To insert a hyperlink to a place within your workbook:

1 Select the cell you want to place the hyperlink in.

2 Click **Hyperlink** in the **Links** group on the **Insert** tab.

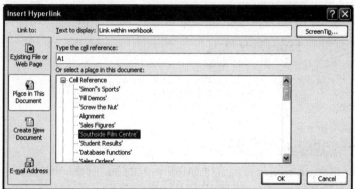

3 Select *Place in This Document* in the **Link to:** options.

4 Enter the text you want on the worksheet in the **Text to display:** field.

5 Enter the cell reference, or select a place from the list.

6 Click **OK**.

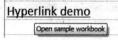

- ScreenTips are useful when you want to provide information about a hyperlink. A ScreenTip is displayed when your mouse hovers over the hyperlink.

- Click **ScreenTip**, enter the text for the tip in the dialog box and click **OK**.

To insert a hyperlink to a place on the Web:

1 Select the cell you want to place the hyperlink in.

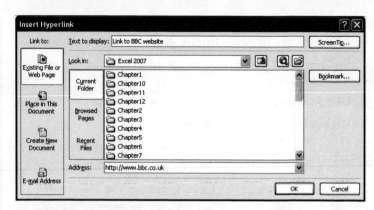

2 Click the **Hyperlink** button in the **Links** group.

3 Select *Existing File or Web page* in the **Link to:** options.

4 Enter your display text.

5 Type in the **Address** of the page you want to jump to.

Or

6 Click 🔍 to browse the Web.

7 Locate the page you want to link to.

8 Return to Excel – click Microsoft Excel on the taskbar.

9 Click **OK** at the **Insert Hyperlink** dialog box.

To insert a hyperlink to an e-mail address:

1 Select the cell you want to place the hyperlink in.

2 Click **Hyperlink** in the **Links** group on the **Insert** tab.

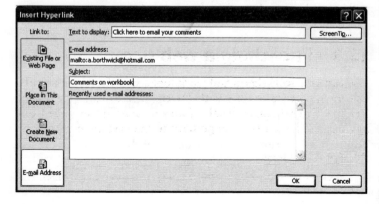

3 Select *E-mail Address* in the **Link to:** options.

4 Complete the **Text to display**, **E-mail address** and **Subject** fields.

5 Click **OK**.

To edit a hyperlink:

1 Right-click on the cell that contains the hyperlink.

2 Select **Edit Hyperlink…** from the menu.

3 Edit the details as required.

4 Click **OK**.

To remove a hyperlink:

1 Right-click on the cell that contains the hyperlink.

2 Select **Remove Link**.

Cut
Copy
Paste
Paste Special…
Insert…
Delete…
Clear Contents
Filter ▸
Sort ▸
New Comment
Format Cells…
Pick From Drop-down List…
Name a Range…
Edit Hyperlink…
Open Hyperlink
Remove Hyperlink

Using hyperlinks

To follow the hyperlink:

1 Point to the hyperlink with the mouse.

2 Click and hold the left mouse button.

3 Release the button.

Once you've jumped to a hyperlink, then returned to your workbook, the hyperlink field changes colour – usually to violet. This will remind you that you've already used that hyperlink.

12.3 Publishing a web page

You can save worksheets and workbooks as web pages and publish them so that anyone with Internet access can view them. Save your workbook as usual before you create a web page from any part of it, then you can go back to the original if necessary.

To save a web page:

1 Open your workbook and display the part to publish.

2 Click the Microsoft Office button and click **Save As...**

3 Select *Web Page* in the **Save as type:** field.

4 Specify the path and filename for your file.

5 Click **Change Title...** to give your web page a title – this will appear in the title bar when viewed in your browser.

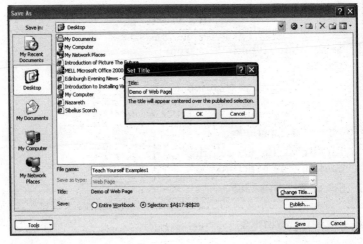

6 Click **OK** to close the **Set Page Title** dialog box.

7 Click **Publish...**

8 Select the data you wish to publish in the **Choose** field.

9 Select **Open published web page** in the browser checkbox.

10 Click **Publish.**

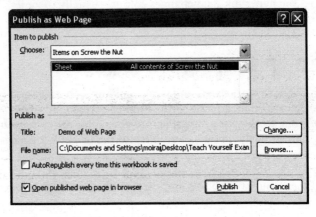

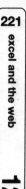

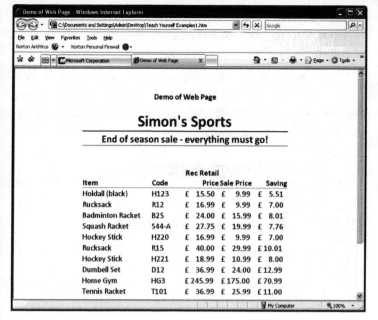

* Close your web browser when you've finished viewing your page.

12.4 Editing your web page

You can easily update your web page as necessary.

To update the workbook containing the data and the web page:

1 Open the workbook.

2 Update as necessary.

3 Save the workbook.

4 Work through steps 2–9 above.

5 Choose **Replace file** at the prompt to replace the outdated file.

To update a web page but not the workbook:

1 Open the web page in Excel.

2 Edit as required.

3 Click **Save** and close the file.

You can open a web page file in Excel or in your browser, from the Open dialog box.

◆ To open the file in your browser to view it rather then edit it, click the **Open** button's drop-down arrow and choose **Open in Browser**.

12.5 Publishing to the Web

To publish your web page to the Web you must copy your file from your own computer to your service provider's server. This will be switched on 24 hours a day, so anyone who knows the URL of your web page will be able to access it at any time.

You may have folders set up in *My Network Places* (on the **Places** bar in the **Save As** dialog box) for your files, or you could publish them to MSN.

Most service providers will allocate some free storage space to you for your own web pages – 10 MB is fairly typical.

There are a number of ways to upload files to a web server – contact your service provider to find out how to upload your files to their server.

If you have created hyperlinks in your web page that jump to other files on your computer, remember to upload all the files, not just the main page.

When you update the workbooks, remember to copy the new versions to your service provider's server and keep your web pages up to date.

12.6 Research

If you create worksheets where you need to research details, you may find the Resarch feature useful. This enables you to quickly reference information on your computer or online without leaving Excel. The research options include thesauruses, translation tools and access to online reference sites.

It's easy to use and you can customize its setting to suit your own research needs.

1 Click the **Research** button in the **Proofing** group on the Review tab.

2 Type in the word or phrase you want to research.

3 Choose your research places from the reference books and sites available.

4 Click 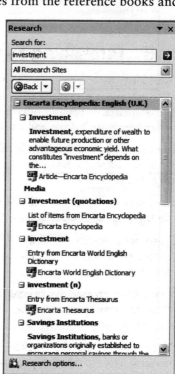.

• The results of the search will be displayed in the **Research** panel.

5 Scroll through the panel and read any articles that take you interest.

To customize your Research options:

1 Click **Research Options...** at the bottom of the Research panel.

2 Choose **Add Services...** and add any links – you can copy and paste URLs from the Internet.

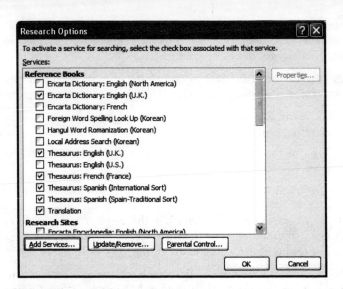

3 To update or remove services, click **Update/Remove...** and amend your information.

4 Click **OK** to close the **Research Options** dialog box.

Summary

This final chapter has discussed ways in which you can interact with the wider world from Excel. We have covered how to:

- Send e-mail messages and faxes

- Create hyperlinks to other files, to places in a workbook and to web pages

- Display a user-friendly prompt for hyperlinks

- Edit web files

- Find out about publishing your web pages

- Search the Internet or your network from within Excel.

taking it further

If you've mastered half of what's in this book, you are well on the way to becoming a proficient Excel user. If you are getting to grips with most of it, you are doing very well indeed.

You'll find lots of information on Excel on the Internet, in addition to the **Help** menu option **Microsoft Office Online** that takes you to their web site.

You could also try searching the Web for sites that provide information on Excel Try entering "Microsoft Excel" + "Software Reviews" into your search engine. You should come up with several sites worth a look.

If you would like to join a course to consolidate your skills, you could try your local college, or search the Internet for on-line courses. Most courses cost money, but you may find the odd free one – try searching for +Excel + tutorial + free.

Good Excel skills are useful on many levels – personal, educational and vocational. Now that you have improved your Excel skills, why not consider going for certification? The challenge of an exam can be fun, and a recognized certificate may improve your job prospects. There are a number of different bodies that you could consider.

You may want to consider Microsoft Office Specialist exams or ECDL (European Computer Driving Licence) – basic or advanced certification. Or, if you feel more ambitious, how about other Microsoft Certified Professional exams?

Visit **http://www.microsoft.com/learning/mcp/officespecialist/ requirements.asp** for information on MOS certification or **http://www.ecdl.com** for information on ECDL.

index